MARKET
STREET
PASTOR

MARKET STREET PASTOR

*Ministry Sustainability
without Money Stress*

ERIC HOKE

Foreword by Peyton Jones

RESOURCE *Publications* · Eugene, Oregon

MARKET STREET PASTOR
Ministry Sustainability without Money Stress

Resource Publications
An Imprint of Wipf and Stock Publishers
199 W. 8th Ave., Suite 3
Eugene, OR 97401

www.wipfandstock.com

PAPERBACK ISBN: 979-8-3852-1984-1
HARDCOVER ISBN: 979-8-3852-1985-8
EBOOK ISBN: 979-8-3852-1986-5

VERSION NUMBER 092324

To my daughters, all my love, Dad

Contents

Foreword by Peyton Jones

THE WORLD HAS SHIFTED. You can feel it. Since Covid, 30 million Americans have not returned to church. But this isn't the real reason to embrace marketplace ministry. The true joy of marketplace ministry is the reach that it affords ministers who truly want to place their finger on the pulse of the people in their community. If you're looking to find a guidebook for those who want to enter the marketplace like the Apostle Paul, then Eric Hoke's book should be your next purchase.

—Peyton Jones,
Author of Church Plantology and Founder at New Breed Training

Chapter 1: The Mindset

"If people knew how hard I had to work to gain my mastery, it would not seem so wonderful at all."

—MICHELANGELO

HOW DID WE GET HERE?

I HAD JUST ACCEPTED a role as a Youth Pastor at one of the largest churches in my denomination. I was thrilled to finally break into the megachurch world. As a budding pastor in my mid-twenties, I thought I was leaving behind the small church life with its low salaries and low status.

After saying goodbye to a great church and a special season of ministry, my wife and I packed all we owned (which was not much) into a box truck and made the trek to our new home for my new role.

Everything was perfect, until it wasn't.

Due to unclear expectations in the interview process, the pastor decided five days into my employment that I was not the right fit and fired me on the spot.

He demanded that I sign a non-disclosure agreement (NDA). It stipulated that I could not come on church property, and that I could not share what had happened with anyone from the congregation. If I did not sign the NDA, we would have to leave the church parsonage immediately.

Not knowing what I know now about housing or employment laws, I signed the NDA which bought me 2 more weeks to figure out what was next and where my family was going to live.

I was terrified. Like many people in ministry, I had trusted the word of the pastors and people in my denomination that this was the right career move—more money; bigger church; larger influence.

I bought that belief, hook, line and sinker and it had cost me, massively.

I will share more details from this story as this book progresses. For now, I want to start with an observation. Vocational pastors often face low pay and questionable job security, especially in independent and evangelical circles. Just like me, pastors can be fired over disagreements in ministry philosophy.

I have now worked with hundreds of pastors in transition, and I know that my story was an extreme—but not isolated—case. This is why a large part of my work now involves helping pastors and ministry leaders build robust and healthy staff cultures within the church.

I am convinced that not all transitions from pastoral ministry must be this way. Most of the pastors I work with are experiencing grace-filled ministry transitions. But the sticking point remains: if a pastor relies fully on the church to fund life and ministry, does that put the pastor's family, career, and community in jeopardy?

BRYAN'S STORY

Throughout this book, I will share real life examples of pastors that I have coached. Their names and details slightly adjusted. Here is a story of one pastor and his journey from full-time pastor to marketplace leader.

Bryan is a thirty-four-year-old Youth Pastor at a 200-person church in suburban Atlanta. He has walked the traditional ministry route, following the advice of parents, pastors, and mentors. It typically runs like this:

Go to your denomination's Bible college. Attend seminary at that same school. Secure a staff pastor job at a medium-sized church. Once you earn enough credibility, you may become a Lead Pastor, likely somewhere around your mid- to late-thirties.

Bryan grew up in a conservative Christian home. Compliance to norms was celebrated, and Bryan followed the steps to the tee. At Bible college, he earned an undergraduate degree in Biblical Studies, and then stayed for three more years to earn the Master of Divinity degree. During that time, he met the love of his life, Sheryl, who was studying to be a teacher. The stars seemed to be aligning for a long, fruitful life of vocational ministry.

Upon graduation, Bryan and Sheryl relocated to an affluent suburb outside of Atlanta where Bryan began serving as a Youth Pastor to a youth group of forty teens. Sheryl found a job teaching at a local elementary school. As the next 9 years passed, they fell into the routines of adulthood. They worked hard to pay down their mounting student loan debt, and they had two children—a boy and a girl.

Everything was going according to plan, but there was something still deeply wrong.

Bryan struggled to reconcile the realities of his ministry position with their dreams. They were "getting by" financially, but they were nowhere close to thriving. Bryan noticed a widening lifestyle gap between himself and friends and church members who worked traditional marketplace roles.

Bryan thought that he had accepted the fact that choosing to be in full-time vocational ministry meant earning significantly less money over the course of his life than if he had worked in a traditional job. Early on, that did not bother him. But now, as a father approaching his mid-thirties, things weren't adding up. Quality of life gaps that he'd ignored before continued to bother him. He was unable to afford a home in that Atlanta suburb. A decade had passed since graduation, and he was still unable to pay down his student-loan debt. His wife's dream of being a stay-at-home mom would forever remain just that—a dream.

Bryan was beginning to wonder if this truly was the path he wanted to walk down for the next thirty years of his career. He loved Jesus, his family, and being used by God in the local church. But he was beginning to wonder, "What if. . ."

He was at the age now where he could begin exploring the opportunities of becoming a full-time pastor at another church. Yet, they liked where they lived. Their kids were in the local school where Sheryl taught. They enjoyed sitting around the firepit on summer Fridays with friends, telling stories and connecting. They had a meaningful community and had built their lives there. To uproot and move seemed dramatic. Yet he knew that if wanted to look for a full-time lead pastor role, it would most likely require a move to a different city, and possibly a different state. Bryan did not want to do that to his family.

The other pain point in Bryan's story was that he had found that after nine years in vocational ministry, it was not the job that he thought he had signed up for. He felt called by God to full-time vocational ministry because he wanted to preach the good news of Jesus, and disciple people to help them grow in their walk with Him. He loved being with people and journeying with them through the highs and lows of life. Yet most of his days were spent doing administrative work, ordering supplies for the youth room, and organizing volunteers in a church management app. Opportunities to "do ministry" by being with people and sharing the Gospel with them were occasional and rare.

One Tuesday morning, after Bryan dropped his children off at school, he did what he did every Tuesday morning, which was to swing by the local coffee shop to begin another week of administrative work leading up to Sunday service. The long list of Amazon orders, staffing volunteers, expense reports, and scheduling social media posts was before him.

This morning was different. He would normally sit in the corner facing the wall with his back towards the crowd. His reason was always the same: he wanted to focus on the task at hand and not be distracted. This time, he decided to turn himself around and face toward the coffee bar to observe patrons coming in for their caffeine fix before blitzing off to work.

The crowd was eclectic: construction workers, businesspeople, police officers, nurses, stay-at home parents having meetups with their kids tagging along, and the occasional college student also using the space to work.

Bryan's mind started spinning. He wondered, "What would it be like to be one of those people and to have a 'normal' job?"

A small part of him even felt compelled to approach the college student to tell her, "Hey, make sure you are studying what you want to and not just what older people around you told you to."

But Bryan was never that bold.

His fleeting thought of "What if?" was quickly clouded by the reality: "I cannot."

His inner monologue reminded him, "You studied Bible and Theology in college. You have a Master of Divinity for crying out loud. You have spent the last nine years as a Youth Pastor hosting dodgeball nights and pizza parties. You're on a path to become a Lead Pastor in the next year or two. Not to mention—who would even hire you?"

Beyond that, he felt shame for even considering leaving full-time ministry. Wouldn't that be abandoning God's call on his life?

Bryan felt desperate. He loved ministry, he loved Jesus, yet he felt like he was stuck. The corner where he sat that morning reminded him of the corner that he had painted himself into professionally. There was no way he could change now.

Who would hire him? What would he even have the skillset to do? What does the average working person do?

He looked back down at his laptop, pulled open his to-do list for the week, the long list of Amazon orders, staffing volunteers, expense reports and scheduling social media posts, and told himself to just forget it. It would never happen anyways.

At thirty-four years old, Bryan felt professionally stuck.

COVOCATIONAL MINISTRY

I hear a certain kind of story over and over in my work with ihelp-pastorsgetjobs.com. Many vocational pastors hit a certain point in their career where they begin to question whether they can continue being a vocational minister. The COVID-19 pandemic expedited that. In March 2022, Barna Group released a study indicating that 42% of pastors have considered quitting ministry.[1]

Some of the pastors I work with want to leave ministry altogether. Others want to explore a bivocational or covocational model of ministry.

Traditionally, bivocational ministers are ministers who have to work a second job to supplement their ministry income but intend to move into a full-time pastoral role as soon the income from the church can meet their family's needs.

Covocational ministry is a bit different, I personally love Brad Brisco's definition, "A covocational church planter is one whose primary vocation is in the marketplace and at the same time is called to start (or lead) a church."[2]

WELCOME TO MINDSET

I have coached thousands of pastors and career changers in my life and Bryan's story is typical. I will hop onto a video call with a pastor, and he or she will begin telling me their story. Before they even get five minutes in, I already know where it is going to end.

Just like Bryan, the story ends with them desperate to make a change, unhappy with their circumstances and doubtful that they could even do anything different professionally.

One even told me after applying to a dozen marketplace jobs with no callbacks, "I am simply unemployable."

He wasn't even forty years old.

1. https://www.barna.com/research/pastors-quitting-ministry/

2. https://www.newchurches.com/resource/5-reasons-to-be-a-co-vocational-pastor/

CHAPTER 1: THE MINDSET

The most painful part is that they love God, His church and feel the call to be a pastor, but they realize what they are doing is not sustainable. Just like Bryan's story, they are getting by, but certainly not thriving. They are living a story that they do not want to keep living and are unsure how to change.

Whenever pastors like this find me, I always start by telling them that the most important first step is Self-Belief. Until you believe you can change, you won't.

You must believe that the ministry has prepared you with skills that employers want and will pay you to do. Ministry was not a waste, but it was preparation for your next assignment, wherever that may be.

The journey of these pages will teach you how to do that. It is not a quick or easy process. It will require you to test your assumptions, and rethink many of the models that you have been taught are normal for ministry. It will also require you to find your confidence again.

Because of the challenges of long-term vocational ministry, most of the pastors that I work with are confused about what else they can do, viewing themselves with extremely low self-regard. The ministry has beat them up. Because the prevailing model of "success" for churches often celebrates "The Three B's" (buildings, budgets, butts in the pews), pastors come to me emotionally depleted.

This has always fascinated me. I would imagine that any person who decided to become a full-time pastor must be a person with incredible confidence in God and in their unique calling to be used by Him to make a difference in the lives of others.

I have nothing against any accountants reading this book, but I have never heard an accountant say that they have a divine calling from God to give their life to spreadsheets.

If the confidence is not there, how do you breathe it back to life? If you cannot portray yourself as a confident and self-assured professional, it's impossible to rebrand and secure a new job. The pastors I work with who can't find this confidence never find jobs. The mindset shift must come first.

Some of you are probably thinking: "There are a million reasons why I can't just leave ministry and go work somewhere else!" I am glad that you think that. I don't want you to leave the ministry. I want you to stay in the ministry while working another job.

This is the secret of this book. To be a Market Street Pastor and lead a ministry of sustainability without money stress, you must rethink your ministry paradigm and look at your ministry as covocational.

Building off Brisco's language, "covocational" is someone who looks at all of their life as a ministry. Their church is a ministry, and their job is a ministry. Traditionally, a bivocational pastor tends to be a pastor who works another job because they must. In contrast, a covocational pastor works another job by choice. Scripturally, every Christian is a covocational minister (Ephesians 4:12).

BACK TO BRYAN

We know that Bryan wants to stay in ministry and that he wants to become a lead pastor. We also know that he wants to stay in his immediate community because he has developed friendships, and because he does not want to uproot his family. Yet he is conflicted because he also wants to explore life outside of vocational ministry, expand his earning potential, and (whether he knows it or not) find his confidence again.

The advice that I would give to Bryan—and you, if you can relate to him—is to consider covocational ministry as your next calling.

This book that will help you rebrand your ministry skills, positioning you to find a full-time job that will pay your bills and that could free you up to do the following:

- Pastor a smaller church that cannot afford a full-time pastor.
- Start your own ministry driven by your passions and interests.
- Plant your own church without having to fundraise your salary.

- Serve at a larger church as a lay minister, supporting a pastor.

- Begin a house church or micro-church for your family and non-church-going friends.

The Kingdom-possibilities for Bryan are endless, but he has many pressing problems. Primarily, these problems include:

- Discovering what a non-ministry job could look like, and how to get one.

- Earning more money so that his family can thrive, and not just survive.

Becoming a lead pastor, and staying in his community, can all be solved by one not-so-simple solution. Bryan must go out and get a marketplace job with a background in ministry.

This is the counsel that I give to pastors who sense that they are stuck, desperate for a change, but with no idea where to start. This sounds great but there are endless whataboutisms when it comes to making the change and I hope to address some here.

FRAMEWORK: BLOCKS AND RELEASES

There is an endless list of myths that pastors believe about why they cannot pivot out of full-time ministry—or at least consider the covocational option. Whether you are reading this book because you want to explore covocational ministry, or because you just want out of ministry altogether, here are five blocks and releases that can help bring clarity to the most popular myths pastors believe about themselves.

Objection 1: I Don't Have Time

- Block: I don't have time to work outside the ministry. I am too busy. I work 70+ hours a week, and mostly dealing with crises.

- Release: As a pastor, you are called to equip the saints to do the work of ministry (Ephesians 4:12).

- Behavior: You must give up control, trusting others to do the work of the ministry.

I spent the bulk of my ministry as a covocational church planter with three children under the age of five, living and ministering in the South Bronx of New York City. Church planting, fatherhood, and full-time employment in a major city is not exactly the recipe for slow and easy living, and I will not pretend it is.

As much as I wish I could spend my evenings kicking up my feet in a hammock, sipping on a chilled lemonade while watching the sunset over the ocean, the calling God had for me in that season was about cramming into a smelly subway car, walking through the rain after a 10-hour work day before spending the evening coaxing my children to eat their vegetables, and then getting to bed at a decent hour.

In my calling as a pastor, I had to take the text of Ephesians 4:12 seriously. My primary calling is not to do the ministry, but to equip others to do the ministry. You might think this would be obvious in our churches and taught to us by our Bible colleges and seminaries. Yet the prevailing ministry model continues to emphasize pastors and key leaders who carry the load of ministry while the rest spectate and observe.

Or am I the only pastor who thinks it all relies on him?

The first question you as a pastor must ask yourself is, "Am I willing to give up control and trust others to carry out the work of the ministry?"

If your answer is "yes" then you need to accept that others will never do things exactly how you would want them done. If you are not okay with people doing things differently, then really, your answer to the above question is a "no."

If you decide to pursue covocational ministry, you must be willing to release your death grip grasp over every aspect of the church and the ministry. You must empower others to minister alongside you, and they are going to sometimes get it wrong.

This is the cornerstone of the mindset necessary for covocational ministry. If this framework were a house, this would be the foundation.

You must give up control. Let's be honest, most pastors love being in control.

Objection 2: I Can't Minister Outside a 9-to-5 Work Schedule

- Block: Because of the varied schedule of a pastor, I cannot commit to the forty-hour weekly grind.
- Release: The modern workplace is one of flexibility, work-life balance, and asynchronous work.
- Behavior: You need to create systems that position you to do the best work in all areas of your life.

Whenever I coach the over-functioning pastor, I share with them about phantom busyness. Most of us in ministry are not as strapped for time as we think. Yes, we are always on call, and that makes us feel like we are maxed out on time. But if we took a few moments to audit our weekly activities, we may find out that we are not as time poor as we think.

Here's a simple exercise. Take out a sheet of paper and make three columns.

Column 1—Activities that only you can do as the pastor.

Column 2—Activities that you could delegate.

Column 3—Activities that you do, but simply don't need to happen and can be eliminated.

When I ask a busy pastor to walk me through their three columns, commonly by the end of the conversation a look of shock crosses the pastor's face. They say, "Oh, I get it now. I am simply doing too much."

For most full-time pastors, your workload is spent engaging in activities that could be delegated or eliminated.

Think about how Bryan was about to spend his Tuesday ordering supplies online. Did that sound a bit too familiar?

When you sit down with a pen and paper and begin auditing your activities, it becomes glaringly obvious that many of the tasks that you do have nothing to do with your core responsibilities as a pastor.

How many of your day-to-day activities advance the mission of your local church? How many of your well-polished Facebook ads—that you spent an hour fine-tuning—converted to people showing up on a Sunday? Some churches may have found great success in this and good on them, but for most of us, very little fruit has come from those activities.

Here are three activities that you should look at closely in your weekly cadence to see if you can make changes.

1. Sermon Prep: Pastors (especially church planters) who spend 20–30 hours a week writing a weekly sermon should reconsider if that is the best use of their time. Unless you are the teaching pastor of a large church, delivering world class sermons every week that are going to be disseminated all over the globe, there's no reason you cannot write your sermon in one day (or two half days). Typically, all you need is 5–8 hours.

2. Administrative Work: Whether it is scheduling social media posts, typing up the weekly bulletin, ensuring volunteer slots are filled for Sunday, sending email blasts, or updating the website, the list of to-dos never ends for pastors. How many countless hours a day do you spend doing administrative work that could be given to a volunteer or group of volunteers or contract a Virtual Assistant group? This one change will free you up to focus on the work that God has wired you to accomplish that will move His mission forward.

3. Counseling, weddings, and funerals. I know some pastors who live for this stuff—so let me share my thought process. I am not a licensed counselor, so I refer people to one. If they cannot afford one, our church would help pay for one. I made

a rule for myself that I will only perform marriages and funerals for people in my church, but no one else. My rationale is simple. My time is limited, and I must focus on what God has called me to do. He didn't call me to be a minister-for-hire. Besides, I hate wearing suits.

When you begin freeing yourself from the unrealistic duties that you may have assigned to yourself (or that culture has assigned to you), your schedule will start opening.

Now, how do you cram a job into the mix?

The thought of being chained to a desk for forty hours a week terrifies most pastors. Apart from manufacturing and the service industry, that way of working is dead and will never come back.

The jobs that I recommend in Chapter 2 are in the knowledge economy. The definition of a "knowledge job" varies, but essentially you are paid for your expertise, not your time.

The story is told of a man who kept hearing a strange sound on his boat engine and could not figure it out. He called a boat mechanic who drove to the dock and listened to the sound. He then reached into his toolbox, squeezed tight into the engine, reached his hand down, and gently tapped a small lever back into place.

He asked the owner to fire up the boat and the sound magically stopped. The delighted boat owner asked, "How much?"

The man replied, "$200."

The shocked boat owner asked, "$200?! You were here for less than 5 minutes!"

The boat mechanic replied, "You are not paying me for the time it took me to fix your engine, you're paying me for the time it took me to learn how to fix your engine."

I love this story because when you break into the knowledge economy, you are not tied to a desk for forty hours a week. You are paid for your expertise. Thankfully, as a pastor, you have tons of that.

Objection 3: I'm Not Qualified

- Block: I have no industry background to get hired since all I have ever done is work in churches.

- Release: Messaging your transferable skills is not only doable, but necessary and this book will teach you how.

- Behavior: Begin to identify what skills you have gained in ministry that are transferable to the marketplace career you would like to pursue.

This one fascinates me because I would think that people who chose to enter ministry have a high sense of self regard, but in the reality of church work, it got lost somewhere along the way. Mindset shifting is where the confidence that you may have buried has to find its way back into the forefront of your mind and heart. You must accept that God has called you to do something incredible in your life and ministry, even if your ministry is small and unassuming like most of ours are.

A few years back I had a conversation with a senior leader in my organization about moving into people management. Though I decided that was not the path for me, she asked if I had ever managed anyone before in the corporate setting.

I had not, and she was surprised. She told me I was a "natural leader."

I told her, "This may be a bit of over-sharing, but I am heavily involved in my church. So, although I have never managed in the corporate environment, I have managed teams of volunteers my whole adult life. I worked in a church where I was the director of the children's program and had a volunteer staff of forty with tiered levels of leadership: directors, team leaders, and front-line staff. Managing volunteers is significantly more challenging than managing paid employees, because they must want to be there. Paid staff have their livelihood tied up with performing their duties. Volunteers are there by their own volition."

She laughed and responded, "This makes a lot more sense now. Why didn't you ever tell me that you did that? You are being so under-utilized at this company."

I share that story because you have stories like that from your ministry experience as well. You will share these once you begin interviewing for roles. In Chapter 4, I will discuss interviews and how to communicate your transferable skills. If you want to skip ahead, go right on and do it. I don't mind.

Whether you recognize it or not, your skillset mix is vast and complex. I have never met a pastor who thought too highly of himself or herself in this area; we all downplay our accomplishments, skills, and expertise, typically under the guise of false humility.

Selling your "hard" transferable skills is half of the equation. The other half is selling your "soft" skills, which are also becoming known as "power skills" or "essential skills." Examples of these include:

- Collaboration and teamwork

- Communication, written and verbal

- Time management

- Problem solving

- Creativity, resourcefulness

- Conflict management

- Openness to feedback (Anyone who has greeted people at the door after preaching is an expert here!)

You have amassed these skills in your work as a pastor in ways that cannot be taught in a classroom. Do not be afraid to own your achievements. You have earned them, and companies want them.

Imagine yourself, the Market Street Pastor, as bifurcated. On one branch you sell your hard, transferable skills in a way that makes sense to a marketplace hiring manager. On the other branch, you sell your power skills, which you have simply because you have been in the people business and understand how humans operate.

When you see yourself through this lens, with hard essential skills and high people skills, you will begin to be marketable to the marketplace economy. Do you sense your confidence rising yet? You have so much to offer.

Objection 4: I Don't Want to Be Greedy

- Block: Amassing wealth is evil, and I don't want to be vain.
- Release: Providing for your family is scriptural (1 Timothy 5:8).
- Behavior: Write down your personal philosophy of pastoral compensation, with vivid detail on why you should only receive your income from the church.

When I sensed that God had called me to ministry at a Baptist church as a seventeen-year-old, I did not have the capacity to process all that may or may not entail. Since I was born into a supportive family, no one ever sat me down and said, "Hey this ministry stuff is great. . . but how are you going to financially support a family one day?"

At the time, I would have responded glibly, "I don't have a need for money. I trust God to provide for all my needs."

Effectively, that means, "I trust God's people to provide for all of my needs through their generosity."

For the next ten years, I viewed amassing wealth as an evil to be avoided. I would internally question the Christian commitment of church members who took exotic vacations or drove fancy cars like a Toyota Camry. I would think of myself as better than other people because I didn't worry about such carnal concerns as buying new shoes, a winter jacket, or health insurance.

God always did provide. He did not do so because of my robust philosophy of pastoral compensation, but despite my serious lack of one.

The church members that I judged for their exotic vacations or new shoes were the same church members who funded my salary. They were the same people that woke up every weekday morning and showered, shaved, brushed their teeth, got their kids out of the door for school, worked eight-plus hours, and did it all again the next day.

They were the same people that were generous enough to donate a few hours on their only one or two days off a week to come to church and serve.

I realized that I had a judgmental view of them. I thought I was better than them because I did "spiritual work" and they did "secular work." That low view of earning money in the marketplace remained a huge blocker until I recognized that all work can be godly work when the intent behind it is to glorify Him. Yes, even used car salesmen can do godly work.

When you think of your own "calling" story, and you begin writing down why you should only receive your compensation from the church, you will quickly realize that the script given to you was perhaps not informed by Scripture. Instead, you carry assumptions about how ministry should work and how ministers should be paid.

I have worked with lots of pastors, and I cannot recall many conversations where the person on the other end of the phone told me, "I want to get a new job so I can buy a Tesla or a second home."

Most pastors that I speak to simply want to provide the best life possible for their families, without the stress of low ministry wages.

Objection 5: Covocational Ministry is an Admission of Failure

- Blocker: Covocational ministry is for those who couldn't quite hack it.
- Release: Covocational ministers are not 'half' ministers, they are 'twice' the ministers because they have a ministry in their churches and in the marketplace.

- Behavior: Begin to dream about what 'all of life as ministry' could look like for you as a pastor.

When I planted All Saints Church in 2017, a distant relative saw me at a family gathering and commented, "Eric, I see that you entered the ministry."

He had a look of pride in his eyes, like I had just joined the Marine Corps.

I thanked him for his comment and had a slight chuckle to myself, because his view of 'the ministry' involved a church or parachurch organization in a formal position, normally as a paid member of the staff.

The paradigm we read in Scripture is that all of God's people are in ministry. There are no "special forces" of Christians and regular civilians. Remember, all Christians are covocational ministers.

The concept of covocational ministers as the "junior varsity of ministry" stems from the wrongly held belief that ministry is reserved for the paid pastors and church leaders. The 'bigger is better' mentality combined with the "3 B's" creates an expectation that full-time ministry is the elite, and everything else is just second class. Foolish!

Any pastor who can simultaneously disciple a team of disciple makers to function as a church while also holding down a job is a hero, not a failure.

WHAT CAN I DO NOW?

I hope this first chapter inspires and challenges your thinking. Maybe, like Bryan, you've wondered "who would hire me" or thought you were unemployable. I hope you can remove those thoughts from your mind, by God's grace.

I love ministry and I know that ministry can beat a person up. It can make them second-guess their abilities and lose their confidence. Just remember that if confidence can be lost, it can also be regained. I hope this book helps you find yourself again.

What I want you to do now is go to ihelppastorsgetjobs.com and download our free PDF about the "Top 10 mistakes pastors make when transitioning to the marketplace and how to avoid them." This free document and the subsequent emails that follow will begin expanding your imagination of what could be.

I wrote this for the Bryans of the world, and imagined them sitting in the corner of the coffee shop wondering, "What would it be like to be one of those people and to have a 'normal' job?"

This isn't a book about leaving ministry, but about expanding your ministry beyond the four walls of the church to a ministry of sustainability without the money stress. Let's go on this journey together.

YOUR NEXT STEPS:

1. Can you relate to Bryan's story and mindset? Do you struggle with self-belief? Has your time in ministry lowered your personal confidence in what you can do professionally?

2. What 'scripts' do you believe about covocational or bivocational ministry that need to be confronted? Do you sense that it is unmanageable for yourself to expand your ministry in this way?

3. What would you do for God if money wasn't a limiting factor? In what ways is only earning a ministry income keeping you from living the life and making the impact you desire?

Chapter 2: Discovery

"The vast majority of us go to our graves without knowing who we are.
We unconsciously live someone else's life, or at least someone else's
expectations for us. This does violence to us, our relationship with God,
and ultimately to others."

—Peter Scazzero

WHO AM I OUTSIDE OF MINISTRY?

I hope that you left Chapter 1 with a glimmer of hope for the
possibilities when you expand your ministry options beyond the
status quo. Whenever I coach pastors through a vocational transition, a recurring theme is a deep sense of hopelessness. They
wonder, "Can I actually do this?" Pastors often doubt their own
abilities, and another insidious fear reinforces these doubts: "How
can I get any hiring manager or recruiter to even pay attention?"

Chapter 3 is all about The Rebrand and in that section, you
will learn how to market yourself in a way that makes sense given
your professional background.

But before we face outward, we need to face inward.

You may be wondering what I did after I lost my church job,
signed the NDA, and had two weeks to find a new home for my
family.

The first thing I did was cry. The pressure and pain of my situation overwhelmed me. After I was done being a puddle of emotion, I began job searching. I found a role as an Admissions Counselor at the seminary where I was in the process of finishing my degree.

When I applied, I knew that this would not be my "forever job." It was a "bridge job," which is a role that you perform for six to eighteen months while searching for a position that better fits your skills and requirements. I lasted exactly six months in this role; it ended when my whole department was downsized. Let me tell you, that was a great year professionally.

After securing that role, I found a healthy church where I could worship, Redeemer Presbyterian Church at their West Side location. The very first Sunday that I worshiped there, I went to the front for prayer from one of the deacons. I shared my story with an older man who listened and prayed. It was a healing moment. To this day, I cannot walk into that church building without feeling incredible gratitude for the community that I found during an incredibly low point.

The man who prayed for me also led a Tuesday morning men's breakfast group that met at 7:00 a.m. for bagels, conversation, and prayer. I also joined this group, where I met some other Christian men in the church. I was able to open and share my story with these men, and I received prayer, support, and encouragement. These men even helped my wife and I move into our apartment. Praise God for His church!

I share all of this because I fear that so many pastors have negative experiences in a local church that they disconnect from the church at large. That is never the right approach. If you were harmed by people, you can only be healed by people. When I had my unjust termination from a church, the place where I found healing and hope again was the church.

RITCHIE'S STORY

Ritchie was a forty-four-year-old pastor and church planter in a historically underserved community in a small town. After eight years of faithful ministry in this community, his church was still nowhere near being self-sufficient. The outside funders were beginning to pull back from supporting Ritchie's fledgling church startup. As he approached a decade of ministry, there was not much to show for it other than a few dozen faithful members.

Despite Ritchie's deep sense of calling to his community and the people who called his church home, he was feeling stuck. With a growing family and increased financial need, the low wages that the church could afford to give him were not enough to make ends meet.

When I first met Ritchie, I listened to his story, and it was evident that he was at a breaking point. He had no interest in continuing to fundraise for his church plant, knowing that the harsh reality was many large donors would view his congregation as a risky place to put their money. He did not want to leave his ministry for a larger, more established church in another part of the country. Given the nature of the community where he lived, jobs were sparse. He thought his only options were driving a school bus or becoming a teller at the local bank.

I began our meeting by asking Ritchie about his passions and what fired him up about his ministry.

He told me about the vision that God had given him to start his own congregation in a difficult and overlooked section of his home state. He shared how much he enjoyed being out in the community, meeting small business owners and families, hearing their stories, and sharing his own.

He told me about one experience that he was proud of was from a few summers prior. His church had hosted a "giveback week" where mission teams from all over North America ascended into his community. They beautified community parks, painted a public middle school, and hosted a block party at the end of the week. One surprise from that event was that the mayor presented

Ritchie with a key to the city, expressing deep gratitude for his church's work in the betterment of the neighborhood.

Ritchie was a natural connector who cared deeply about people and was oriented towards action.

As Ritchie finished sharing his heart, my response was, "You are a natural salesperson, and should pursue a job in sales!"

Ritchie balked at the idea, characterizing salespeople as creepy low lives who get rich by ripping people off. I assured Ritchie that people like that do exist, but true sales are just meeting a need. I told him that if my pipe burst at two a.m. and started flooding my house, I would not care if the plumber sold me his service. The plumber would be meeting a need, and I would pay a lot of money for him to rush over.

After a few months of career coaching, Ritchie did end up breaking into the sales world. He knew he wanted to sell software and work remotely, since his town did not have many options for in-person roles.

He secured a remote job as an Account Executive at a small technology firm based out of Austin. He earned $65,000 per year plus commissions, and he had health insurance for his wife and three kids, as well as other benefits. He still leads his developing congregation and has begun to deploy more volunteers to carry the extra load of ministry. He is investing more into his associate pastor, who is also covocational, and they are still doing great work in his community.

Most importantly, the pastor that I met on that first phone call who was at his breaking point, mentally and financially, is gone. Ritchie has newfound confidence that he can lead his church into its next season of health, sustainability, and longevity.

One of my favorite details from Ritchie's story is that he had two offers come in around the same time, and he picked one over the other. The hiring manager for the company he did not pick called him and asked, "What would it take to change your mind?"

This is a pastor who was breaking into software sales. He had no prior experience in this field and had impressed the hiring team so much that the manager was asking him to reconsider. Who says pastors do not have transferable skills?

WELCOME TO DISCOVERY

Ritchie's journey is not rare, and I expect that you could identify with some pieces of his story. One of the mistakes that Ritchie made was that he began his job search with the local market demand, without considering his skills, passions, and interests.

A person like Ritchie would have hated driving a school bus or working as a bank teller, simply based on God's wiring for his life. This may sound counterintuitive, but you need to start by thinking about yourself—and not the job market—as you begin to think through what types of jobs you would like to pursue.

Before you begin checking Indeed and before you refresh your LinkedIn profile, you need to ask yourself, "How has God wired me as a person? Based on that wiring, what types of jobs should I look for?"

If you decide to make a leap into a new role that you despise because it does not align with your wiring, you are defeating the purpose of this book's core teaching. The whole concept of the Market Street Pastor is ministry sustainability without money stress. To spend forty hours a week in a job that causes you stress will not lead to sustainability.

The other reason why it is so critical to understand yourself is that if you do decide to pursue a covocational model of ministry, you need to be crystal clear on what ministry tasks and assignments you want to focus on in your work in the church. See Chapter 5 for more.

Just as the centerpiece of the chapter on mindset was self-belief, the centerpiece of discovery is self-awareness. Do you know what you are good at, what you enjoy doing, and what a company would pay you for?

The framework for discovery is simple. It starts from within and understanding yourself, what you are good at, what excites you and what you can get paid to do. I created this framework as an easy-to-remember tool to help you quickly self-identify what career direction God may have created you to pursue. I call it the "Head-Heart-Hands-Feet" method.

THE HEAD

If you are a person that would self-identify as academic, cerebral, or "in your thoughts" often, you may be more of a "head-oriented" person. If you enjoy reading, writing, researching, and wrestling with complex ideas—including making difficult concepts simple and accessible—there is a whole lane of professional functions that I would suggest.

When I meet pastors like you who possess a deep intellect, and a capacity not only to learn but also to teach and explain concepts to groups, my immediate suggestion is to pursue a career in Learning and Development.

The first career path that somebody could explore for Learning and Development is that of a Facilitator, Instructor, or Trainer. According to a 2022 survey, 91% of Learning and Development professionals had the core skill of training as their primary job function.[1] Typically, Learning and Development sits within the Human Resources team and requires deep collaboration with people managers and senior leaders to assess staff needs.

The core duties can vary depending on the role, but some of the most common training topics will include the following:

- Onboarding new employees to the company: Onboarding is the process of integrating new employees into the organization. It involves familiarizing them with company policies, procedures, culture, and their role within the organization. Effective onboarding programs aim to facilitate a smooth transition for new hires, helping them to feel welcome, prepared, and equipped to contribute to the company's success.

1. https://360learning.com/guide/learning-and-development-career-path/learning-and-development-career-path/

- Skill development programs such as feedback or time management: Skill development programs focus on enhancing specific competencies or abilities crucial for job performance. Examples include programs on providing and receiving feedback effectively, time management techniques, communication skills, leadership development, and problem-solving. These programs aim to empower employees with the skills needed to excel in their roles and advance their careers.

- Safety and compliance training: Safety and compliance training programs ensure that employees understand and adhere to safety regulations, protocols, and legal requirements relevant to their work environment. These programs cover topics such as workplace safety procedures, emergency protocols, health regulations, and industry-specific compliance standards. The goal is to mitigate risks, promote a safe work environment, and ensure legal compliance.

- Diversity, Equity, and Inclusion (DEI): DEI training initiatives aim to foster a workplace culture that values and respects diversity, promotes equity, and embraces inclusion. These programs raise awareness about biases, discrimination, and systemic inequalities, and provide education on creating an inclusive and equitable work environment. DEI training helps organizations cultivate diverse talent, foster innovation, and create a more welcoming and supportive workplace for all employees.

- Training employees in new technologies: With rapid advancements in technology, organizations often provide training programs to help employees adapt to new tools, software, or systems relevant to their roles. These programs may include technical training on software applications, cybersecurity awareness, data privacy regulations, or emerging technologies. Training employees in new technologies ensures that they remain proficient and effective in their job roles amidst technological advancements.

- One-to-One Coaching (1:1): This involves personalized guidance and support provided to an individual employee by a professional coach or mentor. This approach focuses on the specific needs, goals, and development areas of the employee, offering tailored feedback, advice, and strategies for growth and improvement. One-to-one coaching sessions typically involve regular meetings between the coach and the employee, fostering a supportive and developmental relationship aimed at enhancing the individual's performance, skills, and career progression.

If Learning and Development strikes you as an interesting path to explore, begin writing down answers to these questions while searching for a Learning & Development role:

- Do I enjoy working with people and helping them develop their skills? Learning and development professionals need to enjoy working with people and have a passion for helping them develop their skills and knowledge. Consider whether you have experience teaching, training, or coaching others, and whether you find this work rewarding.

- What skills and expertise do I have in learning and development? Learning and development requires a range of skills, including instructional design, facilitation, coaching, and evaluation. Consider your skills and expertise in these areas and whether you have a background in education, instructional design, or related fields.

- What are my long-term career goals and how does learning and development fit into them? Consider how a career in learning and development fits into your long-term career goals. Are there opportunities for growth and advancement in this field that align with your interests and expertise?

- Am I comfortable with technology and able to stay current with new tools and platforms? Learning and development often involves the use of technology, such as learning management systems and e-learning tools. Consider whether you are comfortable with technology and able to stay current with new tools and platforms.

- Do I have strong project management skills? Learning and development often involves managing complex projects, such as developing training programs or implementing new learning technologies. Consider whether you have strong project management skills and can manage timelines, budgets, and stakeholders effectively.

- What types of organizations am I interested in working for? Learning and development professionals work in a variety of settings, including corporate, nonprofit, and government organizations. Consider what types of organizations you are interested in working for and how their learning and development needs differ.

- What is my approach to problem-solving and innovation? Learning and development often involves developing creative solutions to problems and leveraging new technologies and approaches to improve learning outcomes. Consider your approach to problem-solving and innovation, and whether it aligns with the demands of the learning and development field.

This is a neatly transferable skill set for you as a pastor. You have trained volunteer staff, lay leaders, board members, and mission teams throughout the course of your career as a pastor. Translating those skills may be tricky, but I will explain how to do that in Chapter 4 when we dive into the interview process.

Certifications can also be a great way to bolster your resume and build your professional brand. There are multiple professional certifications that you can pursue to become a Learning and Development Facilitator:

- ATD's Certified Professional in Talent Development (CPTD): Formerly known as the Certified Professional in Learning and Performance (CPLP), this certification is offered by the Association for Talent Development (ATD). It validates professionals' expertise in talent development, including areas such as instructional design, training delivery, performance improvement, and evaluating learning impact.

- HRCI's Professional in Human Resources (PHR): This certification, offered by the Human Resource Certification Institute (HRCI), is designed for HR professionals who have experience with program implementation, have a tactical/logistical orientation, are accountable to another HR professional within the organization, and are generally involved in HR operations.

- HRCI's Senior Professional in Human Resources (SPHR): Also offered by HRCI, this certification is intended for HR professionals who operate primarily in a strategic role, have extensive HR experience, provide guidance to senior management, and possess comprehensive knowledge of HR policies and procedures.

- SHRM Certified Professional (SHRM-CP): Offered by the Society for Human Resource Management (SHRM), this certification is for HR professionals who are engaged in implementing policies and strategies, serve as point persons for staff and stakeholders, and have responsibilities that include HR operations.

- SHRM Senior Certified Professional (SHRM-SCP): Also offered by SHRM, this certification is designed for HR professionals who operate primarily in a strategic role, have broad HR responsibilities, contribute to the development of HR strategies, and have leadership roles within the organization's HR department.

Possessing a working knowledge of the following tools and techniques will only propel your odds of securing a Learning & Development role.

- Adult Learning Principles

- Designing Instructional Material utilizing the ADDIE Approach
- 4 Levels of Evaluation - The Kirkpatrick Model
- Learning Management Systems
- Human Resource Management Systems
- Content Authoring
- Video Editing

The soft skills required for a Learning and Development role are as follows:

- Research Skills
- Communicating to large, small, and 1:1 audience
- Organization and time management
- Adaptability and agility
- Passion to learn that is contagious

If you read this list and sense that you are a "head-oriented" person, I would suggest searching for roles with these titles and begin writing down the recurring themes:

- Learning and Development Manager
- Learning and Development Coordinator
- Learning and Development Facilitator
- Learning and Development Specialist
- Corporate Coach
- Corporate Trainer
- Enablement Trainer
- Instructional Designer

For what it is worth, Learning and Development is the path that I chose after transitioning from full time vocational ministry. I do not consider myself particularly academic, but I do enjoy training people, and love to work with them through their professional challenges. It has been a good fit for me.

THE HEART

If you are a person that is compassionate, caring, giving, and found yourself crying at the end of Encanto, then you may be a heart-oriented person. A heart-oriented person is someone who loves caring for people, hospital visits, and simply the 'ministry of presence.' You are someone who has your heart tug when you pass a homeless person, or senses deep conviction of life's injustices.

When I meet pastors like you who have a high degree of compassion and care for people, I suggest that you explore nonprofit jobs. In my view, this is the easiest "off-ramp" from full time vocational ministry as churches are nonprofits and nonprofits tend to employ religious people who want to make the world a better place.

Nonprofit work is an industry, and there are dozens of paths under the general umbrella of this line of work. Here are a few:

- Fundraising and development. If you love meeting donors, hearing their stories and tying their needs into the needs of the nonprofit, I suggest exploring a fundraising or donor development role. This is a secure nonprofit job, since you are adding revenue to the organization and its goals. However, it can be high pressure. You will likely have a fundraising target within a given timeframe.

- Program and Project Management. This can encompass lots of different functions, and nonprofits tend to be lean. Wearing multiple hats is the norm (not that you've ever had to do that as a pastor). Program and Project Management tends to be a "catch-all" for everything from volunteer mobilization, collaboration with external vendors, leading meetings, and (as the name implies) managing programs. This can be a great place to start if you are interested in project management (the hands) at a for-profit and would like to prepare yourself for that move.

- Direct Service. Typically, when this language is used in non-profits, it means you are working directly with the primary stakeholder. For example, if you are in direct service for an organization that provides meals for the elderly, you are delivering or serving those meals. If the nonprofit mentors teenagers, you are the person actually mentoring the teen-ager. This is the most challenging type of role, but also tends to be the most fulfilling. Unfortunately, these critical roles also tend to be the lowest paid.

- Executive or Senior Leadership. If you love being the person at or towards the top of an organization, pursue senior roles in nonprofits. Like being a lead pastor, you would manage multiple priorities, typically including reporting to a board, strategy, vision, and representing the agency to outside part-ners and the public.

If nonprofits strike you as an interesting path to explore, be-gin writing down answers to these questions while searching for a nonprofit role:

- What causes and issues am I passionate about? Nonprofit organizations are often dedicated to addressing social, envi-ronmental, or cultural issues. Consider what issues you feel most strongly about and whether you would find fulfillment in working to address them.

- What skills and expertise can I bring to a nonprofit role? Nonprofit organizations require a wide range of skills, from fundraising and program management to marketing and communications. Consider what skills and expertise you can bring to the table and how they might align with the needs of different nonprofit organizations.

- What is my work style and how does it align with the culture of nonprofit organizations? Nonprofit organizations can vary greatly in their culture and work style. Consider whether you prefer a more collaborative or independent work environment, and whether you thrive in fast-paced or more relaxed settings.

- What are my salary expectations and how do they align with the nonprofit sector? Salaries in the nonprofit sector can be lower than those in the for-profit sector. Consider whether you are comfortable with the salary range typically offered for roles in the nonprofit sector and whether you are willing to make this trade-off for the opportunity to work for a mission-driven organization.

- What is my career trajectory and how does a nonprofit job fit into my long-term career goals? Consider how a job in the nonprofit sector fits into your long-term career trajectory. Does it align with your career goals? Are there opportunities for growth and advancement within the nonprofit sector that align with your interests and expertise?

- What is the organizational culture and values of the nonprofit organization? It is important to research the organizational culture and values of the nonprofit organization that you are considering. Do their values and culture align with yours? Do they have a positive reputation in the community?

- How much do I know about the organization and its mission? It is important to research the nonprofit organization and its mission before considering a job. What is the organization's history, what are their goals and objectives, and how do they aim to achieve them? Knowing about the organization and its mission can help you determine if the organization is a good fit for you.

Certifications do exist for the nonprofit world and can be found through higher education or certifying bodies. The CNP (Certified Nonprofit Professional) often emerges as the "Gold Standard" for nonprofit professionals who want a competitive edge while job seeking. The CRFE (Certified Fundraising Executive) is great for those who want to pursue development or fundraising.

Like all other lines of work, there are a variety of certifications you can explore if you sense nonprofit work is in your future, especially if you desire a leadership role. My counsel here would be to focus on "harder skills" before necessarily exploring a Nonprofit Management Certificate. Though there is always validity in learning, I have yet to come across a nonprofit that viewed that credential as a deal-breaker or dealmaker. Here are some of the primary players in that space:

- Certified Nonprofit Professional (CNP): This certification recognizes individuals who have acquired the necessary skills and knowledge to excel in the nonprofit sector. It typically covers areas such as nonprofit management, fundraising, program development, and advocacy.

- Certified Nonprofit Executive (CNE): The CNE designation signifies a high level of expertise and leadership in nonprofit management. Holders of this certification often have extensive experience in leading nonprofit organizations, managing teams, developing strategic plans, and ensuring effective governance.

- Certified Nonprofit Consultant (CNC): This certification is for professionals who provide consulting services to nonprofit organizations. CNC holders have demonstrated proficiency in areas such as nonprofit management, strategic planning, fundraising, board development, and program evaluation, enabling them to offer valuable guidance and support to nonprofits.

- Certified Fundraising Executive (CFRE): CFRE is a globally recognized certification for fundraising professionals. It validates the expertise of individuals in various aspects of fundraising, including donor relations, prospect research, grant writing, and fundraising planning. CFRE holders are skilled in implementing effective fundraising strategies to support the mission and goals of nonprofit organizations.

To propel your job search in the nonprofit space, begin volunteering in agencies and organizations that you would like to work in. There are dozens of types of nonprofits but the four most popular are charities, religious institutions (what you are currently doing), private foundations and political organizations. If you sense this is the space you want to explore, begin volunteering at some of your "dream" nonprofits. Even massive nonprofits have opportunities to volunteer, and as I will share in Chapter 3, networking is the name of the game to find a new job.

As you begin to volunteer and build your reputation as a professional, you can bolster your resume and begin networking and applying. Applying to nonprofits is unique, because they normally don't have the means to post roles on places like LinkedIn and Indeed. Instead, they may use idealist.org and workforgood. org. These sites only post nonprofit roles. This is especially true of smaller nonprofits.

Also, check the websites of companies that interest you, often they only post jobs there. The primary job functions that nonprofits need vary, but here are some good places to start:

- Accounting / Finance
- Administrative / Clerical
- Advocacy / Lobbying
- Development / Fundraising
- Direct Service / Social Service
- Education / Teaching
- Executive / Senior Management
- Human Resources / Recruiting
- Legal
- Marketing / Communications
- Program / Project Management
- Public Policy / Administration
- Research

- Social Work / Counseling
- Volunteer Services

Possessing a working knowledge of the following tools and techniques will only propel your odds of securing a nonprofit role:

- Grant Writing
- Fundraising
- Branding
- Project Management
- Financial Management
- Event Planning
- Marketing
- Social Media
- Copywriting
- Researching
- Volunteer Engagement and Development

Finally, the soft skills required for a nonprofit role are as follows:

- Passion for the Cause
- Empathy
- Emotional Intelligence
- Creativity
- Collaboration
- Cultural Competency

If you read this list and sense that you are a "heart-oriented" person, I would suggest searching for roles with these titles and begin writing down the recurring themes:

- Director of Development
- Major Gifts Officer

- Corporate Giving Manager

- Grant Writer

- Chief Executive Officer (CEO)

- Chief Financial Officer (CFO)

- Chief Compliance Officer (COO)

- Communications Director

- Program Manager

- Special Events Manager

- Volunteer Manager

- Membership Manager

- Donor Relations Manager

If you sense that this may be a path you want to explore, the greatest value you can bring to position yourself as a prime candidate is first the passion for the cause, followed by the skills that are tied to increasing the nonprofit's revenue. Nonprofit revenue typically comes from two activities: direct income (such as grant writing and fundraising), or through volunteer mobilization. Any professional who wants to set themselves apart in this work must showcase both passion for the cause and the ability to grow revenue.

Nonprofits (at least good ones) will rarely hire someone who does not have passion for the cause and who is not willing to work hard to achieve the organization's goals. Nonprofits exist to serve the good of their client base.

As a pastor, you have done this. You have shared the Gospel with people with real passion and rigor, pointing them to the ultimate story of Christ. You have also organized capital campaigns and special offerings because as a pastor, you know how to do more with less. This is the easiest "off-ramp" from full-time vocational ministry. Churches are nonprofits, and nonprofits tend to employ religious people who want to make the world a better place.

I have worked in nonprofits, large and small. Though they come with unique challenges, you can put your head on the pillow at night knowing that you have done good work.

THE HANDS

If you're a person who likes to "get your hands into things" by way of weekend projects around the house, implementing a new technology into the church, or just mobilizing a group of volunteers to have a chili bake off on the last Sunday in October, then you may be best suited to explore a career in Project Management.

Often when I describe the Project Management profession to pastors, they are shocked that it is actually a job. "It sounds exactly like what I do as a pastor. . . minus the Jesus part." In some ways, that is true. Some may disagree, but the essential skills of a project manager overlap with the essential skills of a pastor. This is especially true of communication and stakeholder engagement, which are the most crucial skills of an effective project manager.

There are a few variants within project management that you can explore:

- Project Manager - This is typically the person who acts as a liaison between the project team (the people carrying out the work) and the stakeholders. Stakeholders could be anyone, from senior leadership to external vendors to end users (or customers). I call the Project Management skill "the hands" because they are always juggling different demands and expectations, and they are skilled in moving the work forward while tempering the expectations of outsiders. Does this sound a bit like church work?

- Project Coordinator - This is a junior role that may support a Project Manager or Project Team. The functions may vary, but generally this is more of an administrative role that ensures the Project Manager has the support that he or she needs to move the project forward. This is a great role for a detail-oriented person who perhaps aspires to the Project Manager position who needs to get a foot in the door.

- Portfolio Manager - This position is typically one step above a Project Manager. While a Project Manager may be working on multiple projects simultaneously, the Portfolio Manager oversees all the Project Managers who are moving all the projects forward. This role would exist in a company with a mature PMO (Project Management Office) and is a senior level position. However, if you have been a pastor of a larger church, network, or denomination, then you have been a Portfolio Manager.

- Agile Project Manager / Scrum Master—Found predominantly in the tech space but rapidly expanding to other industries, the Agile Project Manager or Scrum Master is a similar role to a traditional Project Manager. Unlike traditional project management, agile and scrum methodologies execute projects in an iterative process. If you are interested in working in a fast-paced environment that is constantly changing, this could be worth exploring.

If project management strikes you as an interesting path to explore, begin writing down answers to these questions while searching for a project management role:

- Do you have a strong understanding of project management methodologies and tools? Project managers need to have a solid understanding of project management frameworks, methodologies, and tools. These include Agile, Scrum, Waterfall, and project management software.

- Do you have experience managing projects or leading teams? Project managers need to have experience leading teams and managing complex projects. If you have experience in a related field, such as engineering, construction, or IT, you may be well-suited to become a project manager.

- Do you have strong communication and interpersonal skills? Project managers need to be able to communicate effectively with stakeholders, team members, and clients. Strong interpersonal skills are also crucial for building relationships, managing conflicts, and resolving issues.

- Do you have strong organizational and time management skills? Project managers need to be highly organized and able to manage multiple tasks and priorities effectively. You should be able to plan, prioritize, and execute tasks and projects efficiently.

- Are you a strong leader? Project managers need to be able to lead and motivate their team members, set goals and objectives, and hold team members accountable. They should also be able to delegate tasks and responsibilities effectively.

- Are you able to manage risk and uncertainty? Project managers need to be able to anticipate and effectively manage risk and uncertainty. They should be able to identify potential risks, develop contingency plans, and make decisions in uncertain situations.

- Are you comfortable with data analysis and reporting? Project managers need to be able to analyze data and provide accurate and timely reports to stakeholders and team members. You should be comfortable with data analysis tools and reporting software.

- Do you have a strong work ethic and the ability to work under pressure? Project managers need to be able to work independently and under pressure to meet project deadlines and deliverables. You should have a strong work ethic and be willing to put in the time and effort required to deliver high-quality results.

Finding a project management job is incredibly overwhelming. At the time of this writing, there were 50,000 project management jobs in the United States posted on Linkedin. . . in the last week.

Since the skills of a project manager remain consistent across industries, I would suggest that you begin by identifying what type of company you want to work for, and it's almost certain that they could use a project manager.

In terms of professional certifications, the Project Management Professional from Project Management Institute remains the most popular. Here are a list and short descriptor of the different Project Management certifications you can earn:

- Project Management Professional (PMP): Offered by the Project Management Institute (PMI), PMP is one of the most widely recognized certifications globally. It demonstrates competency in leading and directing project teams.

- Certified Associate in Project Management (CAPM): Also offered by PMI, CAPM is an entry-level certification for project practitioners. It demonstrates understanding of fundamental project management concepts, terminology, and processes.

- PRINCE2 (PRojects IN Controlled Environments): A process -based method for effective project management, PRINCE2 certification is widely used in the UK and internationally. It focuses on dividing projects into manageable stages.

- Certified ScrumMaster (CSM): Offered by the Scrum Alliance, CSM focuses on the Scrum framework, an agile methodology for managing complex projects. It is ideal for those involved in Scrum teams as Scrum Masters.

- PMI Agile Certified Practitioner (PMI-ACP): Also offered by PMI, PMI-ACP recognizes knowledge of agile principles and practices. It demonstrates the ability to apply agile methodologies to project management.

- Certified Project Manager (CPM): Offered by the International Association of Project and Program Management (IAPPM), CPM certification covers a broad range of project management skills and knowledge.

- Professional Scrum Master I: Offered by Scrum.org focused on delivering agile projects in organizations.

- Certified Project Management Practitioner (CPMP): Offered by the Global Association for Quality Management (GAQM), CPMP is designed to assess project management skills and knowledge.

- Six Sigma Green Belt/Black Belt: While not strictly project management certifications, Six Sigma certifications demonstrate proficiency in process improvement methodologies that are often applied in project management contexts.

If you sense that project management may be a path worth exploring, I advise learning how to frame projects that you have done in ministry in a way that would make sense to a person who is not familiar with church work.

In short, a project is a container of work with a beginning and end point, typically with multiple people involved. For example, writing a sermon or counseling someone would not qualify as a project since there are typically not multiple people involved in carrying out the work (unless you have a sermon development team).

Here are some sample projects you have done as a pastor without even realizing it:

- Community Outreach Projects
- Vacation Bible School
- Volunteer Celebrations
- Special Events in the Church Calendar
- Social Justice Initiatives
- Short Term Mission Trips

All of these would qualify as a project, and you want to be able to describe them as projects. Think about who was involved, how was the communication planned, how much did it cost, and what was the result? Answering those questions will help frame the important work you have done.

The list below is the transferable skills that are required for project managers and possessed by pastors and ministry professionals.

- Leadership: Project managers need strong leadership skills to motivate and guide their team members, inspire confidence, and facilitate collaboration toward achieving project goals.

- Communication: Effective communication is vital for conveying project expectations, status updates, and addressing issues. Project managers must communicate clearly and concisely with stakeholders, team members, and other project participants.

- Organization: Project managers must be highly organized to manage multiple tasks, timelines, and resources efficiently. They need to prioritize activities, allocate resources effectively, and maintain project documentation accurately.

- Time Management: Time management skills are essential for project managers to meet deadlines and keep the project on schedule. They must allocate time wisely, identify critical path activities, and proactively address delays or bottlenecks.

- Risk Management: Project managers need to identify, assess, and mitigate risks that could impact the project's success. They must develop risk management strategies, monitor potential threats, and implement contingency plans to minimize negative impacts.

- Problem-solving: Project managers encounter various challenges during the project lifecycle. They must be adept at analyzing problems, identifying root causes, and developing creative solutions to overcome obstacles and keep the project on track.

- Negotiation: Project managers often need to negotiate with stakeholders, team members, vendors, and other parties to resolve conflicts, secure resources, or address issues. Strong negotiation skills are essential for achieving win-win outcomes and maintaining project alignment.

- Adaptability: Projects are dynamic, and project managers must adapt to changes in scope, requirements, resources, or constraints. They need to be flexible, resilient, and open to adjusting plans or strategies to accommodate evolving project needs.

- Budget Management: Project managers are responsible for managing project budgets, ensuring that expenditure aligns with approved plans and delivering value within budget constraints. They must track costs, control expenses, and make informed decisions to optimize resource utilization.

- Team Building: Project managers play a crucial role in building and nurturing high-performing teams. They must foster a positive team environment, promote collaboration, leverage team strengths, and effectively address conflicts or performance issues.

- Stakeholder Management: Project managers interact with various stakeholders, including clients, sponsors, vendors, and end-users. They must understand stakeholder expectations, engage stakeholders throughout the project lifecycle, and manage communications to ensure alignment and support.

- Quality Management: Project managers are responsible for delivering quality outcomes that meet stakeholder expectations. They must establish quality standards, monitor project deliverables, and implement quality assurance processes to ensure that project objectives are met satisfactorily.

Project management can be a high-stress, high-stakes job with lots of moving parts, competing priorities, large budgets, and often unrealistic expectations from stakeholders. However, if you feel like you are at your best when you are juggling competing demands and bringing people together to unite around a mission, project management can be worth exploring.

CHAPTER 2: DISCOVERY

THE FEET

If you are a tenacious person who likes to stay active (and was possibly medicated as a child for hyperactivity), I would recommend exploring the world of sales. Salespeople get a bad rap amongst church folks because we equate sales with sleaze. But in my view, nothing could be further from the truth. If you are selling a product or service that a person needs at a fair price and of good quality, you're helping make the world a better place.

I also love sales for pastors because whether you want to admit it or not (and most do not), you have done sales.

Think about it. When you're preaching a sermon on Sunday, what are you doing? You're likely using techniques such as persuasion, emotional buy-in, and reason to convince a person that a life following Jesus is better than a life not following Jesus. You're not selling a product or service, but you're selling an idea, a belief, and a conviction. You're communicating the most important message in the world.

Still unconvinced? How do you get people in your church to volunteer for projects? Staff the kid's ministry? Give to a building campaign? Go on a mission trip? You "sell" the idea to them that it is in their best interest to do so. Before you skip this section, let me share two exciting things about sales. As a career changer, sales are not as hard to break into as you may think. Sales is also the most lucrative job in this chapter.

Do I have your attention now? Let's keep reading.

Here are three types of sales functions that are worth understanding if you decide to dip your toes into a role like this:

- Hunter Sales Persona - Sometimes you will see job titles such as Field Sales Representatives or Account Executives. These professionals spend a significant amount of time traveling to meet with clients and prospects face-to-face as well leveraging LinkedIn. They often sell high-value products or services that require personalized presentations and negotiations. This is the type of job for someone who can build rapport and trust quickly. This is a tough job, but if you can do this well,

45

you are incredibly valuable to a company. Some companies pay their top sales reps more than they pay their executive leaders. As a hunter, you are looking for new business, new accounts and bringing in new deals. Companies value this skill, and will compensate you well for it.

- Farmer Sales Persona—If you see titles such as Customer Success, Account Manager, Customer Service Representative, this is likely a farmer role. In these roles, you are not hunting new business, but you are making sure that the current client stays happy and keeps buying your service or product. You are nurturing the relationship, and you are the point of contact for any issues that may arise. This is also a critical role within a sales organization because losing a major client can cost the company greatly. This is a great role for someone who enjoys the long-term relationship aspect of business. As a farmer, you are cultivating, gardening, and watering existing relationships to ensure they continue to grow and be healthy. You do not experience the same pressure as a hunter, but you still have to be willing to keep relationships warm by maintaining communication lines.

- Trapper Sales Persona - The trapper role may be a combination between sales and marketing because the trapper is a content creator that lures in new leads by walking with potential clients in every stage in their journey by soliciting testimonials and reviews, building trust with prospects, and educating potential customers. Potential job titles for a Trapper Sales role may be Sales Associate, Director of Marketing, Marketing Manager, Marketing Specialist. This is a great role for someone who enjoys being creative, has a deep understanding of human behavior and psychology, and has no problem doing "social selling." Social selling means creating marketing collateral that draws in new people. As a trapper, you seek to understand your ICP (ideal client persona) problem and position your product or service to solve that problem.

If sales strike you as an interesting path to explore, begin writing down answers to these questions while searching for a sales role:

- Why do I want to pursue a career in sales? Understanding your motivation is crucial. Are you attracted to sales because of the potential for high earnings, the opportunity for growth, or a genuine passion for sales and persuasion? Believe it or not, in some companies, just saying you want to make as much money as possible is good enough, but others really want to see a passion for the product or service being sold.

- Do I have the necessary skills and traits? Sales requires specific skills and personality traits, including communication skills, resilience, empathy, persuasion, and a competitive spirit. Assess whether you possess or can develop these attributes. This would be a great question to ask your family and friends. Sales is not for everyone, and that is OK. Be sure you're prepared for lots of rejections, and ready to bounce back after pitfalls.

- Can I handle rejection and pressure? Sales often involves rejection and pressure to meet targets, often called quotas. Can you cope with rejection and maintain your motivation during challenging times? In any given month or quarter, you may be expected to hit a certain number. Does the pressure of those goals scare you or excite you?

- Do I have a "ramp" of cushion to cover expenses? Your income can be variable, especially in the beginning. It all depends on where you work and how your commission is structured. Some jobs offer a fine salary and anything else is just gravy on top. Others offer no salary, and you must sell to earn. You must decide what level of risk you want to take on.

- Have I sought advice from sales professionals? Speak to people already working in sales to gain insights into the field. They can provide valuable advice and realistic expectations. I would also advise learning sales techniques. It is not just being a smooth talker, but it's about understanding human behavior. I recommend Brand Builders, Sandler Sales and Business Made Simple to learn sales.

Finding a sales job can be tough as there are so many avenues you can explore. In short, if a company sells something, they have a sales force. Breaking into sales of any variety can be a great way to supplement your income and even change careers.

Sales is one of those jobs where results matter more than anything. To share that you fundraised $400,000 in two months for a building campaign will come across significantly better in a job interview than that you amassed multiple sales certifications. However, for those who want to sharpen their sales skills, here are some places to start:

- Certified Professional Salesperson (CPSP): Offered by the National Association of Sales Professionals (NASP), CPSP certification covers fundamental sales skills, including prospecting, communication, negotiation, and closing techniques.

- Certified Sales Executive (CSE): Also provided by NASP, CSE certification is designed for experienced sales professionals looking to demonstrate advanced sales strategies, leadership skills, and industry knowledge.

- Certified Sales Leadership Professional (CSLP): This certification, offered by the Sales Management Association, focuses on sales leadership and management skills, including team building, performance management, and strategic planning.

- Certified Inside Sales Professional (CISP): Offered by the American Association of Inside Sales Professionals (AA-ISP), CISP certification validates proficiency in inside sales techniques, including lead generation, account management, and sales technology usage.

- Certified Professional Sales Leader (CPSL): Provided by the Institute for Professional Excellence in Coaching (iPEC), CPSL certification emphasizes leadership development, coaching skills, and emotional intelligence for sales leaders.

- Certified Sales Operations Professional (CSOP): Offered by the Sales Enablement Society, CSOP certification focuses on sales operations, process optimization, data analysis, and technology implementation to support sales teams.

- Salesforce Certifications: Salesforce offers several certifications for sales professionals, including Salesforce Certified Sales Professional, Salesforce Certified Sales Cloud Consultant, and Salesforce Certified Pardot Specialist, which demonstrate proficiency in using Salesforce CRM and related sales tools.

- HubSpot Sales Certifications: HubSpot provides various certifications for sales professionals, such as HubSpot Sales Software Certification and Inbound Sales Certification, focusing on inbound sales methodology, sales technology, and customer relationship management.

- Miller Heiman Group Certifications: Miller Heiman Group offers certifications such as Strategic Selling, Conceptual Selling, and SPIN Selling, which provide training in sales methodologies and techniques.

- LinkedIn Sales Navigator Certifications: LinkedIn offers certifications for Sales Navigator, its sales prospecting and lead generation tool, demonstrating proficiency in using LinkedIn for social selling and relationship building.

Could you picture yourself as a salesperson? One thing I did not mention about sales that is compelling is the idea of a commission. Most jobs pay you the same amount of money every other week, regardless of how hard or little you work. Sales is different. The harder you work and the better you get at your job, the more earning potential you have. I love sales because anyone can do it and there is not a "type" of person.

Here are the skills you should work on acquiring if you sense that sales is the path you would like to explore:

- Prospecting

- Negotiation
- Product Knowledge
- Closing
- Sales Technology Proficiency
- Relationship Building
- Presentation Skills
- Objection Handling
- Time Management
- Data Analysis

I used to be an awful salesperson, and that was why I did not last long as an admissions counselor at my seminary. Now I run a small business that sells every single day. If I can do it, so can you.

BEHAVIORS

In coaching hundreds of pastors with Ihelppastorsgetjobs.com, I have found the question, "What type of job can I even get as a pastor?" is the top question by a massive margin. At first, I didn't really understand why pastors struggled so much with this, but then I listened to a podcast episode with the late Tim Keller that brought it all into life.

In 2021, David Kinnaman and Carey Nieuwhof interviewed Tim Keller. Tim had been diagnosed with pancreatic cancer, and one of his realizations after his diagnosis was that he was "unfocused." This really surprised me, given the fruit of his ministry in New York City.

This quote stuck with me from that podcast, "And so I should have been more focused, but I was tending to do whatever anybody asked me to do. I'm a nice person, I'm a minister. So you do whatever anybody asks you to do."[2]

---

2. https://careynieuwhof.com/some-thoughts-on-the-life-death-and-legacy-of-tim-keller/

It hit me that as a pastor, you spend a lot of time playing defense. You are meeting the needs of others, caring for them in life's highs and lows. If you are not careful, it is easy to lose your identity as a pastor, because you only know how to operate in response to other's expectations.

As a result, I created a free assessment where you can take about 10 minutes to answer some questions that help you understand what type of leader you are, and where your next role professionally may be. E-mail me at eric@ihelppastorsgetjobs.com and I will send it over to you.

After taking the assessment, spend time thinking through the actions below.

YOUR NEXT STEPS:

1. How has God wired me? What type of work makes me come alive and brings me energy and joy? How can I find a role that taps into that part of me?

2. Who in my personal life can I talk to about my interest in pursuing other employment that could give me honest feedback on my strengths and growth areas?

3. Should I schedule a free discovery call with I Help Pastors Get Jobs to understand more of what is out there and how I can take my next step? (I think yes)!

Chapter 3: Rebrand

Make a radical change in your lifestyle and begin to boldly do things which you may previously never have thought of doing or been too hesitant to attempt. So many people live within unhappy circumstances and yet will not take the initiative to change their situation because they are conditioned to a life of security, conformity, and conservation, all of which may appear to give one peace of mind, but nothing is more damaging to the adventurous spirit within a man than a secure future.

—JON KRAKAUER, INTO THE WILD

1 Timothy 3:1:—"The saying is trustworthy: If anyone aspires to the office of overseer, he desires a noble task."

THE GRAND CANYON SIZED GAP

I AM A BIT of theological mutt, but if you had to pin me down to one tradition, I would be a Baptist. If you know anything about Baptists, you will know that we love Charles Spurgeon. He is like our Lebron James. Any Baptist preacher worth his salt will have Lectures to My Students on his bookshelf, and rightfully so.

More than once, I heard a preacher or professor attribute to Spurgeon with saying, "If God calls you to be a pastor, don't stoop to be a king."

If you have been in ministry for any time, you have heard similar variations of that throughout your life.

I am not here to poke fun at Charles Spurgeon or anyone else who has said or believed similar ideas. I get it. If 1 Timothy 3:1 holds true, the psychological barrier to move from a full-time pastor to a marketplace professional is a large as the Grand Canyon.

Many of us in full-time vocational ministry wrongly believe that we are the elite Navy Seals of Christians, and that Joe the used car dealer and Sally the hairdresser who attend our church are just the 'normal folk.' This type of thinking hurts people, and especially damages the souls of pastors.

We may not come out and say this, but in many of our churches there is a pecking order where the clergy are on the top and the regular working person is on the bottom. Sometimes we even use language like, "they are called to the ministry" as if ministry were some exclusive club. This neglects passages like 2 Corinthians 5:18, which says "all this is from God, who reconciled us to himself through Christ and gave us the ministry of reconciliation." Every Christian is called to ministry.

This returns us to the Grand Canyon-sized psychological barrier. You might think, "I felt called by God to do this, but I am scared and uncertain and don't know if I even can. How do I even go from pastor to marketplace professional? Who would hire me? A pastor?"

At this point in this book, you may be asking yourself, "How in the world do I do this? Just driving past an office park or the high-rise buildings downtown freaks me out. I can't work in one of those, I've only ever worked in churches."

You may be wondering, "If I make this switch, am I a sellout? Am I abandoning God's call on my life by reading this book?"

You might feel a little bit of guilt or shame for thinking about this. The word "rebrand" comes across as icky and gross. It sounds so corporate and slick, but this is what you are doing as a pastor moving into the marketplace.

"God has called me to full-time ministry," you may reason, "I'm not going to stoop to be a king or a queen," as Spurgeon would say.

Let me provide you with some perspective. If God has called you to ministry, does that mean that God has only called you to receive your compensation from the church?

Read that twice if you need to. You may need to think about it. And if you really sense in your heart of hearts that God has called you to only be in full-time vocational ministry forever, may I ask who told you that? How would they react if you were to go knock on their door and say, "I can't pay my bills. I can't make ends meet. My family is suffocating under the current model of vocational ministry. Can you help?"

If full-time ministers are the Christian elite because they earn their paycheck from the church, what does that say about the faithful saints who go to work every day to pay your salary?

Also, what does that say about the bivocational, covocational and volunteer ministers all around the world and throughout Christian history? It does not take much thought to recognize this pecking order of Christians as a house of cards.

HOW I MADE THE SWITCH

When I was in the thick of trying to figure out how to message my skills as I moved from being a pastor to a marketplace professional, I had more questions than answers, and few guides to point me in the right direction.

One woman who helped me tremendously was a church member named Gigi. Gigi was a Corporate Trainer at a for-profit Learning & Development organization based out of London. Her company had hubs all over the world, including New York, where I lived at the time. I had a passion to plant a church but needed to be covocational to supplement my income. When I shared that need with Gigi, she offered to put my name in for a role at her company to join their cadre of trainers.

I am forever indebted to Gigi and will remain a big believer in being open and honest with people about your material needs. Yes, even within your church when appropriate.

This role was freelance and required a five-day training session on how to become a Corporate Trainer within the brand guidelines of the company. The training was non-paid, and only 60% passed. I bet on myself and used paid time off to take the class, even though it wasn't a sure thing. This was the first big decision I made. I did not believe I had what it took, but I mustered up the courage to find the strength to make myself go and stretch myself beyond my comfort zone.

If I could pass this five-day intensive, I would go on to deliver workshops, training, and coaching for some of the most prestigious Fortune 500 companies in the world. I would be afforded opportunities to speak at companies like Uber, Salesforce, Bank of America, and American Express. It would be my first step into the next phase of my life and ministry. But keep in mind, up until this point, I had only ever worked in ministry.

I had no idea what I was doing sitting amongst Marketplace Professionals in that cohort, all of whom appeared polished, confident and. . . simply not me.

They had a gravitas about them that I did not. I was so out of my depth and scared. I had never even worked a corporate job. How am I supposed to coach others on how to do theirs? I thought that I should just walk outside, get on the subway, and head home. It's never going to happen to me. This was a sample of the self-talk I was having in the week-long intensive. This was the weight I was bearing as I attempted to 'rebrand' from pastor to marketplace professional. So if that is you, I get it.

But I kept showing up. Every morning at 8 a.m., my train would take me from my apartment in the Bronx to Grand Central Station. I would walk through that busy, beautiful train station and feelings of smallness washed over me. If anyone knew who I was, or what I had done professionally, I would have never been invited into this cohort.

The company's office was on East 37th Street in Midtown Manhattan. Every day, as I would ride up the elevator, I had to shake off my massive imposter syndrome, take deep breaths, and tell myself that I could do this, even if I did not believe it. Because of my insecurity, I would shrink in that conference room and not share feedback. I was nervous, tense, and awkward. During breaks, I would hide in the bathroom. I could not even finish my lunch most days due to nerves.

"Fake-it-till-you-make it." That was all I kept telling myself and "keep betting on yourself."

I felt like if they find out that I am a pastor, they are going to laugh me out of this room. Everyone here is so smart, well-kept, with a strong presence and energy, and then there's me—a guy with a Bible degree and a seminary degree who only ever worked on staff at a church and had no real-world experience (or so I thought). That week I put as much energy and focus as I could muster. I worked hard and tried to learn the principles. It was stretching my brain like I was back in Greek 1 at Liberty University (where I earned a D).

I just kept showing up. I kept betting on myself. I kept getting on the train and heading downtown. I kept faking it till I made it. I kept talking to myself in the elevator and getting side-eyes from the other passengers.

On the last day of that training was the assessment. All students were required to give a 45-minute presentation in front of the judges. It was pass or fail. If you don't pass your assessment, you don't get the credential of being a Master Coach. The whole week of training would be for naught. Did I mention it was unpaid too? The pressure cooker was at the highest degree, and I felt myself in it, overcome with anxiety that I may just be wasting everyone's time.

The night before the final morning, I laid out my suit and tie, and stayed up late into the night to rehearse my 45-minute presentation. I was resolved that I was not going to mess this up! To make matters worse, of the 8 candidates on assessment day I was the last person to go. I was able to observe everyone else's presentations.

Some crushed it; some bombed. When 4 p.m. rolled around and my name was called, I just walked up, said a little prayer under my breath, and I crushed it, killed it, nailed it. I don't want to sound cocky, but I was by far the best person in my group. The senior facilitator was so impressed, I passed with flying colors, and I got the job!

I tell you that story because I sensed the Holy Spirit using me in that conference room on East 37th Street in Midtown Manhattan. I sensed the Holy Spirit empowering me to do my job well, and I realized in that moment that the Holy Spirit uses us in church and pastoring, but He also works in the marketplace. God also works in the boardroom, and He also wants to use me in ways that I couldn't even imagine. God works through churches, and that God works through office buildings. To see this, you must rebrand yourself and expand your mindset on what it is that God wants to do in and through you.

This is why so many pastors that I work with lack serious confidence. They have been conditioned and programmed to think this is all they can do, that they have no other options, and that they can't expand their professional life beyond what they have always done. They think no one would hire them. These are all lies that keep pastors and ministry folks trapped in situations that are unhealthy. I sometimes even hear pastors say things like, "I just wish I had a real job."

That always shocks me, because you must have a certain level of confidence to be a pastor. I have never heard anyone tell me; "God has called me to be an accountant" (no offense to accountants). Yet, the reality of ministry can suck the confidence out of a person, especially in some churches that are high-pressure environments where you must keep the church members happy because they pay your bills.

If you are a pastor, you have a sense that God has called you and equipped you to do this work. By the time you come to me, you are beat up, frustrated, and desperate for change, but you don't know how to make it. This is why rebranding matters.

I AM JACK'S CORE COMPETENCY

When I met Jack, he was a former pastor. I met him on the other side of his pastoral transition. After pastoring two churches, he realized that for the sake of his family, he had to leave pastoral ministry—though not leave the faith or the local church. He told me his family was not thriving under the 'fishbowl' of full-time pastoral ministry. For the sake of his family's long-term wellbeing, he made the challenging but necessary decision to change careers and break into the marketplace.

Like many pastors, he made the initial switch by working for nonprofits. His first job hired him to do three things—raise money, recruit volunteers, and build the membership of a youth development organization. In the interview, Jack was asked if he thought he had the skills to do those three things well since he only had ministry experience. He had to hold back his smile, because those three skills comprised most of his job as a pastor, including leading his congregation through a massive capital campaign building project just a few years prior.

Like many pastors, Jack struggled with rebranding. But when he recognized the core skills that he brought to the table, it made the transition that much easier. God used his ministry experience and gifts to propel him professionally.

Jack found his niche in fundraising, marketing, and higher education. He has enjoyed a solid career working in the marketplace, while staying involved in the local church as a lay leader.

One of my favorite thoughts from Jack was that he does not look at life through the lens of "buckets"—compartments for ministry, and "not ministry." This is the challenge ministry leaders have with the idea of a ministry transition. Am I still being used by God if my paycheck is not coming from the local church? I hope you recognize that all of life is a ministry, not just what you do for the church.

Rebranding ministry skills to marketplace skills is not easy. This chapter will require some heavy lifting but keep showing up and keep betting on yourself.

CHAPTER 3: REBRAND

WHAT IS THE POINT?

The big point that I want to share with you in this chapter is very simple:

You can rebrand yourself without losing your soul. If Mindset was all about self-belief and Discovery was about self-awareness, then Rebrand is about self-acceptance. You can accept that you are a loved child of God even if you work somewhere besides a church. Praise God for that.

Are you able to get over this Grand Canyon sized hurdle that thinks you are betraying God's call on your life? If not, it's going to be impossible to present the best version of yourself to hiring managers and recruiters. You need to have confidence, not because you are cocky or self-assured, but because you believe in faith that God has a called you to serve him in this way. You must have faith that he wants to use you beyond what you ever thought possible.

If you apply to every job, interview for every position, and just show up with an attitude that says, "This was my backup plan, I don't want to be here. Church just couldn't pay the bills," you will never get hired. Ever. Hiring managers can sniff out who is enthusiastic about the role and who couldn't care less.

Do you have confidence that this is not abandoning God's call on your life, but that He is moving you into the ministry that He has next for you? If so, keep reading. If unsure, call a friend or schedule a time with us at ihelppastorsgetjobs.com.

STEP 1: THE ELEVATOR PITCH

The elevator pitch is a simple concept. Can you explain who you are professionally in one minute or less?

If you are a pastor, you tend to be wordy and long-winded. You willingly pursue tangents if they involve great stories. I tell you this in love. You need to stop.

When it comes to what you do, clear and crisp communication is the name of the game. There's a reason it's called an elevator

59

pitch and not a cross-country flight pitch. Put down your three -point sermon for a moment and pick up this simple template:

1. Where you are from.
2. A moment of change.
3. Where are you going?

Put on a 60-second timer and answer those three prompts in about 20 seconds each. You're on!

When you start getting into interviews, the very first question the person interviewing you is going to ask you is, "Tell me about yourself." If you do not have a succinct and dialed-in answer, you are going to sink that interview in the first 5 minutes. Spend time doing meaningful story work to figure out those three steps and rehearse, rehearse, rehearse. Then, learn to give an answer without sounding too rehearsed. No pressure!

When I was interviewing for a previous role, the hiring manager asked me, "So what interested you in our company?"

I had a succinct answer that won her over, bringing me one step closer to securing the job. This was my elevator pitch to her:

> "I have extensive experience in nonprofit work and have spent the last four years working in the for-profit space traveling to different companies and sharing workshops on leadership and essential skills needed to thrive in the modern workforce. Given the circumstances of the past year, particularly the Covid-19 pandemic, I realized that I want to get back into the 'heart' work that I deeply enjoy. This is why I wanted to return to not-for-profits and give back to the most vulnerable and under-represented in our society. I sensed this organization melded my two worlds together with a deep care for social justice and equity, while also developing and training leaders. So, when I saw this role I thought that this could be a perfect fit to combine my professional background with my passions, and that is why I am excited to talk to you today."

See what I did there? Beginning, middle, and end. In less than a minute, I had shared with her where I came from, what changed, where I want to go, and why my vision for my next career step fit into this role. The position was offered to me, and it ended up being a fantastic opportunity where I spent several years and grew by leaps and bounds professionally and gave me the pedigree to move into a Director role within that industry.

STEP 2: FORMAT YOUR RESUME TO NOT LOOK PRETTY.

This is the most important section of this chapter. Resumes and cover letters are not exciting, but they are crucial vehicles for communicating your skills, experience and expertise. They must make sense to the decision-maker who will read them.

A common misconception among pastors and career changers is that once they develop a healthy resume, their phone will begin ringing off the hook with job interviews. If that were the case it would be ideal (and I would probably be very rich), but it is not. Your resume and cover letter are documents outlining your experience as your first step in the long process that is job seeking.

I recently came across a role that was a blend of non-profit, learning and development, and people management. It was fully remote and paid $120,000 annually. For an everyday pastor looking for his or her first job post ministry, it would be a stretch job. Let's just explore this unique role for the sake of the exercise anyway.

Reading through job descriptions can be daunting, which is why I deploy technologies like ChatGPT to understand the top 5 needs the job description is asking for. I copied and pasted the Job Description into ChatGPT and asked for the core skills in this role and received this:

- Learning and Development Expertise: The ideal candidate should have at least 5 years of experience in building and leading Learning & Development initiatives. They should have a strong knowledge of training and organizational development theories, learning styles, and learning needs.

- Program Management: The candidate should have experience in program management, including evaluating and providing feedback on learning and development programs. They should be able to develop and manage budgets, set KPIs, and ensure organizational funds are used effectively for employee engagement.

- Training and Facilitation: The candidate should be an engaging facilitator and capable trainer, experienced in delivering impactful people leadership development programs. They should be able to design and develop customized learning solutions and facilitate core training.

- Diversity, Equity, and Inclusion (DEI): The candidate should have at least 2 years of experience integrating Learning and Development work with a DEI lens. They should contribute to the organization's DEI goals and actively work towards creating a diverse, equitable, and inclusive culture.

- Communication and Relationship Building: The candidate should possess excellent communication skills to effectively communicate with staff at all levels of the organization in a remote environment. They should be able to build relationships across the organization and collaborate with colleagues based across the United States.

Now that I know what this job description requires, if I possess the skills, I can reverse engineer it to build out a resume and cover letter that matches the job requirements.

The resume template that I use to help pastors like you rebrand is simple, clean, organized, and boring. Remember, this is your first impression of your potential future employer. Just as when you went out on your first date with the person you would one day marry, hopefully you bathed, put on your best clothes, and presented yourself as someone worth spending the rest of your life with.

The same can be said for applying for jobs. Take time to polish your resume to represent the best version of your professional self. As the saying goes, "You never get a second chance to make a first impression." I cannot tell you the volume of awful resumes I have seen simply because people were lazy and did not want to put in the work to make them shine.

As someone who purchased this book, you have access to my template as part of the MasterClass. If you have not already done so, make sure to e-mail me at eric@ihelppastorsgetjobs.com and download that for free.

Building resumes that get callbacks is a muscle that you can develop, but like all muscle building activities, it takes repetitions and gets easier with time.

Now that we know about the format of a resume, we need to discuss the keywords in a resume. Embedding keywords into your resume is a fine dance. You do not want to force-fit words where they do not naturally go, nor do you want to exaggerate your actual skills and abilities. You want to make sure you are speaking the language that the computer reading your resume understands.

The computer, you may ask.

When you apply for a job on a company website, your resume is being read by an Applicant Tracking System before it ever hits the desk of a human being. That is why you can't write "Led Bible Studies" in your marketplace resume. The system does not have a category for that phrase, and your resume will be immediately discarded before a human ever sees it.

You could utilize ChatGPT by asking the prompt, "What are the keywords in this Job Description that could be used in the Applicant Tracking System?" For our example job, these were the results:

- Learning & Development
- Training
- Facilitation
- Professional Development
- Program Management
- Diversity, Equity, and Inclusion (DEI)
- Learning Management Systems (LMS)

- Organizational Development
- Remote Work Environment
- Communication Skills
- Relationship Building
- Leadership Development
- Performance Management
- Talent Acquisition
- Learning Needs
- Learning Styles
- Training Programs
- Human Resources
- Continuous Learning
- Employee Engagement

This is a great list, and I would make every effort to include these words in my resume where they naturally fit. Remember, never force-fit keywords. Doing so makes your resume look mechanical, and any skilled recruiter or hiring manager can spot someone who is trying to hack the system by padding their resume. Also, if you include a hard skill like "Human Resources" on your resume but you did not even know what an Applicant Tracking System was until 15 seconds ago, then delete it off your resume. You cannot lie about your skills.

I advise job seekers to put a professional summary at the top of their resume. Recruiters and hiring managers will only spend 7 seconds looking at your resume, and you want to ensure that the top ⅓ of your resume is eye-catching and compels the recruiter to keep reading. The top ⅓ should be your highlight reel. You want it to grab the attention of the person reading it, so that they want to continue. This should be tweaked slightly for every job application. As the saying goes, looking for a job is the hardest job out there.

A sample professional summary for this job could be something to the effect of:

Experienced Learning and Development professional with a proven track record of designing and implementing impactful training programs and fostering a culture of continuous learning. Skilled in program management, facilitation, and integrating Diversity, Equity, and Inclusion (DEI) principles into learning initiatives. Strong communicator and relationship builder with expertise in remote work environments and proficiency in utilizing Learning Management Systems (LMS) for effective talent development.

STEP 3: BUILD YOUR POWER STATEMENTS: WHAT TO NOT DO.

When it comes to the rebranding, many pastors face a massive hurdle. They are (rightfully) trained to be humble, to think less of themselves, and to give God glory in all things. Yes, and amen.

If you grew up in a ministry context like me, whenever someone complimented your sermon, you had to respond, "praise God" or "to God be the glory." If you said something like, "thank you; I worked really hard on this and your compliment means so much," then you'd be seen as a prideful schmuck.

Being humble is fantastic and necessary in ministry contexts, yet I have seen it become an Achilles heel when it comes to the job search.

The pastors that I work with send me their resumes with their bullet points, and they outline their tasks and duties with phrases such as "managed staff" or "preached sermons." This is an example of being lazy with your resume.

The problem with those statements is that the person reading your resume will have no idea what that specifically means. Imagine if someone who had worked in sales applied to be your Youth Pastor, and their resume used words like "territory, prospecting, CRM, pipeline." You would read that and think, "I want someone to teach our youth and serve families well, and what on earth is a CRM?" You would be confused, and immediately put this resume in the "no" pile because you cannot even comprehend what they have done. That is how hiring managers feel when they see your uncooked resume.

"Managing staff" could mean you had one part-time secretary (who was also your wife), or it could mean that you had forty full-time employees and three-million-dollar payroll.

"Preaching sermons" could mean that you preached every single week to 1500 parishioners, or it could mean that you were on the preaching team at a 40-person church and preached on holiday weekends when the lead pastor went on vacation to the Jersey Shore.

Those situations require radically different skills and experiences.

Imagine that you are hiring an Executive Pastor to manage your church's finances and volunteer teams. Suppose you received a resume where the candidate said that they "managed the budget" at their last church. That does not tell you anything, and you would be unlikely to bring that person in for an interview. Companies think the same way. They want numbers, data, and details. Show what you have done and show off a little! Be humble, but flex pastor!

BUILD YOUR POWER STATEMENT: WHAT TO DO

If you see a job posting asking for someone who can "implement creative organizational and talent development tools and programs" that sounds like a whole lot of word salad. But broken down into its purest form, they are saying they need someone to implement their programs that focus on developing their talent.

Using the power statement framework, you want to spit back to them what they are looking for. Use this framework to compose the bullet points that describe your work experience on your resume:

Action Verb → Quantity / Frequency → Task / Project → End Result

Now, let's build a power statement that corresponds to our example statement from the job description.

- Action Verb. Well, that is easy, they already gave it to us, so let's say "implemented."

- Task / Project. What programs that helped people did you implement as a pastor? If you were a senior pastor and had a board meeting once a month that included staff development that helped your team grow, perhaps reading a book together or watching a webinar, that would most certainly qualify. Perhaps you also sent articles to your staff on personal and professional development, or you provided one-on-one coaching with young pastors in your network to help them develop their ministry skills and abilities. When you add this element, your power statement becomes "implemented organizational and talent development programs."

- Quantity. Remember numbers, data, facts, figures, and results on your resume are your best friend. A resume that reads, "Led volunteer teams" will get looked over immediately. Sit back and think about it, how many touch points did you have with programs and people in your career as a pastor each month? I think twenty would be a good starting point, let's go back to our power statement: You "implemented 20+ creative touchpoints of organizational & talent development programs monthly."

- Result. Now this power statement is starting to get some legs. What was the result from implementing these touch points with your leadership team, staff, younger pastors, and those whom you have impacted? This is where it can get tough to round out, but if you think about it, those people you invested in tended to stay involved in your church longer, serve more, give more, and engage at a deeper level.

So let's add a clause describing results: "Implemented 20+ creative touchpoints of organizational & talent development programs monthly, resulting in 80% retention of the executive leadership team and emerging leaders.

This power statement will give pause to a hiring manager or recruiter. It suggests that you can do this job well, and that is true. But if you had merely said that you had "managed staff," you would miss a huge opportunity to show off your skills and abilities as a professional. You are missing opportunities because you do not want to "brag." It is okay to brag a bit on your resume.

So, what are you waiting for? Start making some power statements.

TIME TO GET GRITTY: POWER STATEMENTS EXAMPLES

Many job seekers, but especially career changers, get intimidated by describing the jobs they have done in bullet points. Here are some examples to start with. Feel free to add these into your resume, changing the numbers to reflect your skills, abilities, and experience:

- Did you hold outreach and recruiting efforts that helped people find your church?

  Directed and executed 15+ strategic engagement events annually, including marketing and communications plans to 250+ stakeholders in community-based organization, fostering a commitment to organizational metrics and achieving 15% annual growth.

- Did you recruit and develop volunteers, identify their giftings, and release them to ministry?

  Recruited, onboarded, and trained staff (volunteers, contract and paid) of 450-person faith-based nonprofit. These volunteers ran all processes inside and outside the organization,

including leadership development, curriculum design, cross
-department collaboration.

- Did you manage the church budget

  Managed fund portfolio of 200+ contribution accounts, proactively prospecting new donors, resulting in a 42% 5-year
  growth, while effectively managing a budget exceeding 600K.

- Did you manage the church's social media and marketing
  efforts?

  Implemented marketing strategies, designing direct-to-con-
  sumer marketing collateral, and managing press releases,
  resulting in 35% growth in customer acquisition.

- Did you function as an HR person at the church?

  Spearheaded Human Resources initiatives, ensuring compliance with federal and state laws, designing and implementing benefits systems, and leading annual benefits enrollment,
  resulting in a 20% increase in employee satisfaction and a
  15% reduction in turnover.

- Did you engage in staff development for volunteers or paid
  staff?

  Built, developed, and iterated on learning curricula, including modules, webinars, and in-person training for volunteers
  and staff who served 200+ church members.

- Did you run a new members' class for people that are joining
  your church?

  Functioned as the key liaison for onboarding a new member,
  ensuring their assimilation into the culture of the church and
  helping them plug into service in different capacities, resulting in increased retention.

- Did you develop and deliver a small group curriculum?

  Authored and taught curriculum for various studies, enhancing the depth and breadth of the educational offerings, leading to a 20% expansion in educational program reach.

STEP 4: EDIT YOUR RESUME BY DROWNING YOUR DARLINGS.

I had one pastor that I was working with who had planted a church in the 1990s. He was now looking for a marketplace role and asked me to create a resume for him. When I gave him his new, updated resume, he was annoyed and offended that I did not include the church that he planted thirty years ago. I explained to him that he had to be discriminatory about what he included on his resume—this was not a job to coach church planters, raise money, or even in the ministry space at all. He insisted that the church that he founded thirty years ago must be included, so I put it on his resume. To no surprise to me, he never received a call back for an interview.

Why? Every single word on your resume needs to fight for its life to be there. If it is not relevant to the job, scrap it. Be liberal with that delete button. Drown your darlings. If those words are not building a case for you to receive a callback for a job interview, they are irrelevant and need to be removed.

I am proud that he planted a church, and I am sure God is too. But hiring manager Jillian and recruiter Keith do not care about something you did in a different industry thirty years ago.

The resume template that I use is not fancy or exciting, but it gets callbacks and invitations to interviews. Remember, your resume is not your ticket to the job, your resume is the ticket to the first interview. You can expand on your experience once you get in the room, but you need to get in the room first.

STEP 5: WRITE THOUGHTFUL COVER LETTERS

Not every job requires cover letters, but we are going to assume you need one. If it is ever optional to upload a cover letter, do not be lazy and skip uploading one. As a career changer, this is the prime opportunity for you to shape your story and build your case explaining why you are applying for this job at that company.

A cover letter should be neat, simple, and match the formatting of your resume. Use my downloadable template to emphasize everything you shared in your resume. Imagine it to be the teaser for the teaser. A cover letter is a carefully crafted document that outlines why I am the best fit for this role. This is short, succinct, and the hiring manager or recruiter can read it in 15 seconds. It is not a big deal at all.

Now the bad news: a polished resume and cover letter are merely a small building block in the foundation of your professional brand. Many career changers mistakenly think that they can just get a well-developed resume, and they will be on their way to the job of their dreams. Not so fast there, partner.

You cannot submit a resume and then sit back, twiddle your thumbs, and wait for the phone to ring or the inbox to chime. Creating and sending a resume is the first step, and there are many more steps to go. If you stop your job search by simply applying to any old job, you will never get a job—or at least, not any time soon.

STEP 6: NETWORK (JUST DON'T BE WEIRD)

Networking is hard but necessary work to secure your next opportunity. This is especially true as a career changer trying to position yourself as the best fit for a role. So how do you do it well especially if you need to be subtle that you are changing careers?

As a godly person like a pastor, I am almost certain you have never wandered into a nightclub in your life. But for the sake of illustration, just imagine that we are going to a nightclub tonight. If it makes you feel better, it can be a sanitized nightclub where they only serve grape juice and play Christian rap (or as the old heads call it, Holy Hip Hop).

I have never been to a nightclub either, but from what I have seen on TV, it appears that there are two primary ways to get into a nightclub. The first way is waiting in a long line for your turn to get to the bouncer who may or may not let you in the door. Normally there is a velvet rope and, in the movies, the people in the line are never wearing jackets, which seems incredibly uncomfortable in the winter.

That is how most people seek a job. They see a job that looks interesting (the night club), so they fire away a resume (stand in a line) and then they wait for the bouncer (a recruiter) to maybe give them a chance to come in the door. It's passive, frustrating, and painful to simply wait around with the high unlikelihood of even getting in. This is a lousy way to find a job, and a lousy way to get into a nightclub (or so I am told). Plus, it's cold and you do not have a jacket.

The second way to get into a nightclub is to be a VIP or know a VIP. If you ever see a movie with a nightclub scene, you may see a Rolls Royce or stretch Hummer limousine pull right in front of the door. Exiting the rear door is a celebrity, an A-lister, someone everyone knows and their entourage of friends. These people by-pass the line, greet the bouncer by their first name, and waltz right into the nightclub with no questions asked.

Who are these people in the job search? They are the people who are at the top of their professional game or have a skill that is in such high demand that companies beg them to bring their talent to their firm. If they are not that, they are friends with people who are at that caliber and have the right connections with the right people. This is called relational capital. If you can get the right person to vouch for your skills, you get pushed to the front of the line.

I am assuming that if you are reading this book, you are not in the top .01% of talent in this new world of marketplace work and will not be waltzed into a job interview with a company begging you to join them anytime soon. That is fine, that was my story too. It is the story for the vast majority of job seekers.

That is why I propose a third way, which is called the side door. Instead of spending half the night standing in line or waiting for a huge break to bypass the line, why not wander around the corner of the nightclub (or job search) and find a side door?

The side door of a nightclub may have a busboy taking out the trash, or a waitress smoking a cigarette, or a chef with the door propped open to get some fresh air. What does that mean for you as a pastor looking for a job? Everything. If executed properly, this side door method will increase your odds of receiving a call back substantially, so do not skimp on this process. Also, do not be weird.

Once I shared this information to a group of pastors, and one man buried his face into his palms because he had been attempting to find a job for years with no callbacks because he was just cold applying. He was standing in the line, cold, irritated and passively waiting for a job to open, which never did.

Before I get too granular, there are a couple of things that are very important before we walk through this process.

First, a resume needs to be dialed-in before you attempt the side door method. If you have a janky and half-baked resume, do not do this as you have not done your due diligence to present the best version of yourself to the hiring manager. You are wasting your time and potentially souring a relationship with someone who could be an advocate for you in getting an interview. Make sure your resume is dialed in and represents you well. We provide resume writing services at IHelpPastorsGetJobs.com so please let us know if we can help you in that way.

The second thing is that when applying for jobs, the goal is not to get a job. I know that sounds strange, but the goal is to get an interview. We will talk about interviews in detail in chapter 4.

So, if I were job searching for a role as Learning and Development Director in Lancaster, PA where I currently reside, I would do a quick search on LinkedIn and see what comes back. Once I found an interesting role, I would carefully read the Job

Description and see if there are any 'hints' indicating who this role might report to.

Typically, a job may read something like, "This role reports to Vice President of Staff Development" or "This role is on the People Operations Team." That is enough intel to figure out who is going to be your waitress or busboy that will get you into the side door.

Instead of merely applying to the job, and waiting for a callback while twiddling my thumbs, I am going to do a LinkedIn Search for the Vice President of Staff Development at the company. Let's assume his name is Pete.

Upon finding Pete, I am going to request him as a contact on LinkedIn. Then what? Well, this is where it gets fun.

While I am waiting for Pete to accept my request, I am going to search for anything I can about the company and their staff development programs and needs. Perhaps it's in earning reports, their social media, or blog. It could be an article someone on that team posted or a press release. The internet is a magical place, so take full advantage.

Suppose I found a podcast that the CEO was on. In the episode, he talks about an emerging talent pilot they are launching to develop their younger staff. I listen to it, take notes, and then do something a bit unorthodox.

I take my cell phone, point it towards my face and create a 60 second video asking the VP of Staff Development at the company I want to work at, "Hi Pete. I am Eric and I was listening to the podcast where your CEO talked about the emerging talent program at your company. He said it was important to the staff development at your company and I was wondering how this open role as a Learning and Development Director will impact that program because I'd love to learn more about that position."

Now let me give you a quick caveat here, because some of your minds are blown reading this.

This technique works great in three circumstances.

- The job is remote, highly competitive, and you have no natural "in" with the hiring manager. If you are stacking your credentials against 200+ other people, many of whom have worked in that industry and have more experience than you, the odds are not looking great. Being a bit 'out there' will help separate you from the pack.

- The hiring manager is active on LinkedIn. Some are and others aren't. Thankfully, you can scroll to someone's LinkedIn profile and see their engagement on the platform. If their page is a ghost town, then it is likely they do not check their messages.

- Large companies such as Fortune 500s. If you tried this with Bob's Custom Patios that employs 80 people, it may work. But at that point, you are probably better off being a bit more traditional, and just giving Bob a call, or swinging by the office to drop off your resume.

If pointing a cell phone towards your face and sending a cold video message is not your cup of tea, you can rely on your network. This is fantastic if you are in a small town where everyone knows everyone. Let's assume this is a local job in a small town, and Pete coaches soccer at the local high school. Now you don't need to know Pete, you need to know someone who knows Pete.

There is nothing wrong with going to your contact and saying, "Hey, I was interested in the role where Pete is the hiring manager. I don't know him, but do you mind introducing us?"

Now I know if you are a pastor, I am aware this can be spicy and dicey, especially if your transition is under the radar. This is also why I am a big fan of being open and honest with your church, staff, and board of your intentions as much as possible. Since the key to a new job is networking and most pastors' entire network is their church, your best bet is to be open, honest, and transparent with all who are in your church orbit. I will share more on that in Chapter 5.

The last way to break into the side door is by networking with people in the company. Suppose reaching Pete is out of the question, but thanks to LinkedIn, you can see who else works there. You may already have a contact there, or a second-degree connection (you know someone who knows someone who works there). That is fantastic! Work on those networks and make some connections. The great thing about reaching out to team members as opposed to hiring managers is that hiring managers get cold messages all the time. Team members do not and are typically more likely to respond.

One last note that you may not be aware of when it comes to networking. Often when people are breaking into the traditional marketplace, they do not realize that current employees are incentivized to refer their friends and family to work at their place of employment. Recruiting and hiring quality people is difficult, and companies know that good people know good people. Therefore, many companies will provide referral bonuses if the person gets hired and stays in the role (typically for 90 days).

So do not think you are being annoyed by networking, or that people are just helping out of the goodness of their heart. Your professional network is eager to pass your name along to the right people, because if you get hired, they get paid. So don't be shy! However, most people are not going to refer a stranger. That is why you need to network your way to your next job. Networking is how you are spending most of your time job seeking. (Read that line twice.)

STEP 7: BUILD A LINKEDIN

For most pastors, LinkedIn is a mysterious website that they do not spend any time on. In fact, most pastors do not even have a LinkedIn account. Yet in the business community, LinkedIn is the preferred social media for professional networking. In this section, I will lay out a simple template for building a LinkedIn profile. This will be easier if you watch it on Masterclass, but let's begin with this important step that you should not skip over if you are flying under the radar while job seeking.

1. Create an account and immediately click on "Settings and Privacy." Make sure the visibility is where you want it to be.

The most important consideration is that your profile updates with your network are toggled off.

The reason is because when people start fine-tuning their LinkedIn, it tends to be a reasonable tell that they are on their way out of an organization. As the joke goes, nothing screams "I am about to quit" more than a LinkedIn refresh. That's not a joke, I just made it up. Come see me next Thursday at Comedy Night.

If you press "OFF," your updates will not be shared with your network as you make them. You also have the capability to block the visibility of certain people. If the church or your elder board is connected to LinkedIn, you can limit how much of your profile they could view.

2. Use a professional headshot. Not a picture of you and your kids, not an iPhone pic of your latest fishing trip pulling in a big tuna. This is your professional brand, and you want it to be represented as such. I personally use an AI-enhanced headshot. There is a cost associated with AI-enhanced headshots, but it is significantly less than paying for professional headshots.

3. Populate your headline, work history, and core skills. Remember, this is your professional brand. If you did the hard work of creating power statements for your resume, you can simply copy and paste them into your LinkedIn profile.

4. Make Connections. The cool thing about LinkedIn is you can sync it to your other contact lists, e-mail, phone number, and other social media. I know some of you may not feel comfortable doing that, but this is a good place to start.

5. Begin posting valuable content. This is the step that many people will skip, but it is so necessary. Only about 1% of people on LinkedIn create posts, making it a prime opportunity to build your professional network and brand. This is not a book on social media strategy, but a good goal would be to

post 3 times a week, hitting 3 areas: entertain, educate, and encourage.

Ultimately, LinkedIn is a place to play offense, not defense. Thinking that a slick profile and a few good posts will land you your dream job is unrealistic. But if you look at it as a piece of your professional brand toolkit, it can be a valuable resource to help you pivot into what God has next for you.

REBRAND CONFUSION

I hope this chapter leaves you encouraged that what you have done in ministry has prepared you well for the marketplace. Here are some final core skills you can utilize in your resumes, interviewing, and networking to talk up your professional accomplishments.

- Empathy—As a minister, I worked with people through some of their most challenging situations and circumstances. This taught me to meet people "where they are" and without judgment.

- Self-Regulation—Leading people through the lens of their spiritual development can be highly stressful, and this line of work is known to lead to burnout. I learned to manage my emotions well, and work in a sustainable manner.

- Self-awareness—Being in a position of religious authority taught me about power dynamics, and the weight of my own words and actions. As a result, I have an astute sense of myself and how others perceive me.

- Cultural Agility—Religious communities welcome people of all backgrounds, and as a result, I learned how to embrace and appreciate different backgrounds.

- Change Management—Leading a congregation through COVID-19 was a massive test of navigating unprecedented change. This experience and other massive changes have taught me how to lead through unknowns.

- Fundraising—The congregation that I founded was funded through the generosity of individuals, organizations, and grants. Being a minister has taught me how to raise and manage funds, and work with a board of trustees.

- Recruiting & Staffing—Throughout my career as a minister, I have recruited, interviewed, onboarded, and off-boarded dozens of staff and volunteers. This has taught me the best practices in finding and developing talent.

- Communication—The core skill of any ministry professional is communication. Preaching is just the beginning. Leading staff meetings, writing copy, and having tough one-on-one conversations have helped sharpen my communication skills and abilities.

- Prioritization and time management—Churches tend to run lean and ministers wear multiple hats, and my career was no exception. This taught me how to empower staff and focus on the highest priority items in my day.

If you are leaving this chapter thinking, "Wow—Mindset had me fired up, Discovery had me inspired but Rebrand has me lost and confused" you are not alone. This is the meatiest chapter in the whole book and in my view, the hardest to articulate in writing. The Masterclass, which is included with the purchase of this book, helps so please e-mail me at eric@ihelppastorsgetjobs.com for your free lifetime access.

YOUR NEXT STEPS:

1. Dial in your Elevator Pitch so that you can summarize who you are and what you do in 60 seconds. Remember, Beginning, Middle, End.

2. Create your Cover Letter, Resume and LinkedIn Profile as outlined in this chapter.

3. Make it a goal to post on LinkedIn with somewhat regularity, remembering this is your professional brand that will be seen by future employers.

Chapter 4: Interviews

"Finally, I am concluding that my highest ambition is to be what I already am. That I will never fulfill my obligation to surpass myself unless I first accept myself, and if I accept myself fully in the right way, I will already have surpassed myself."

—Thomas Merton

HOW I BOMBED THE INTERVIEW
FOR MY DREAM JOB

DURING A JOB SEARCH, the interview is the most important time to be on your 'A-game.' Writing a resume and cover letter is the easy part. You can pad a resume and make it look pretty, but you cannot fake your way through interviews. In the interview, you will be sitting eyeball to eyeball with someone who will be going over your credentials and your qualifications for the role. If applying feels a bit like a game of basketball, interviewing is full court pressure.

One of my children was born with several health complications that were difficult to manage, throwing my world into a tailspin for a few months. During her recovery, I was searching for a job with a bit more income. Yet with everything going on with her health, I was not in the best mental space for interviews.

I applied to one role that would have my dream job at the time—or the closest thing to it then. (I do not think anyone's dream should be tied to a job.) It was like my work as a Coach and Trainer, but it was a full time, hybrid position in New York at an emerging corporate training startup in the Learning & Development industry.

After a rigorous application process, they invited me to a virtual interview. Even though I had three years of experience in the marketplace, I was still getting my bearings. Translating my skills into the language of the marketplace remained a challenge, and I still suffered from massive imposter syndrome. (If you have not noticed, imposter syndrome doesn't go away.) On top of that, the challenges of caring for a child experiencing health challenges during a career move meant that I was not prepared for a job interview that could potentially double my salary.

I logged into Zoom and after some pleasantries with the very kind recruiter, she asked, "So what interests you in this role?"

My brain froze. I began sharing about the health challenges of my child and how I needed to get a full-time job to contribute more to our family. I completely forgot to connect any of this to my relevant skills of the job description. I didn't explain how my skill set could help the company fulfill its vision. As words fell out of my mouth, I could see the recruiter's face drop in shock, confusion, and perhaps a bit of regret for scheduling this call.

Now to give me some grace, in a church interview setting, this would be more appropriate because we hope that in ministry contexts, people can bring more of their "whole selves" to work. But the very first interview for a marketplace job is not the time to share such personal and sensitive information.

The interviewer expressed her thoughts about what I was experiencing in my personal life, and we continued the conversation for thirty more minutes. I received an email a few days later that they would not move forward with my candidacy. They could have skipped the e-mail, because I knew I would not be invited back.

I blew it, and I knew it. I had no one to blame but myself.

This was a critical time in my life and career journey. I had broken through the glass ceiling. I had changed career from full-time clergy to the corporate world. Despite this progress, I had not yet realized into my earning potential in this new industry.

Looking back, I now realize that I was carrying a huge aura of I don't deserve this. Without sharing all the details, the talk track in my brain echoed my impostor syndrome. I thought things like, "I don't deserve to be here," "I am a phony," and "if they knew the real me, they would never hire me." I sometimes wonder if I self-sabotaged that interview because I didn't think that I deserved that job, that title, that compensation, that career leap. I wonder.

BRIANNA'S STORY

When I met Brianna, she was serving as an Executive Pastor of a medium-sized church in a suburban community. She liked her job just fine. The board gave her adequate responsibility, the congregation loved her, and her lead pastor was a fantastic boss and leader. However, after her second son was born, she wanted to make a change.

Her husband had always supported her ministry and was the primary breadwinner in the family. Her role as a staff pastor had a very low earning ceiling, especially considering the hours worked. She told me felt directionless. She knew she wanted to find something where she could work remotely.

Other than being a summer camp counselor, she had never worked outside of vocational ministry. Still, she was confident and set her sights on Project Management. After she earned her Project Management Professional certification, she applied for a few roles.

Once she secured an interview for a Project Coordinator role at an educational company, she scheduled a coaching call with me to practice interview questions. She even sent me the job description. She was on the ball and ready to go.

We got onto the Zoom link together and without missing a beat, I started: "Hi Brianna. I am Eric, interviewing you for the Project Coordinator job. How are you?"

Immediately, her shoulders tensed, and her voice shot up an octave or two. "I'm fine, thanks!"

I smiled and said, "Hey, let's start over."

I advised Brianna to lower her shoulders, relax her voice, and roll her neck if she needed to. Even though Brianna was more than qualified for the job, she was nervous and unsure she could perform in this interview.

A job interview feels like a massive power imbalance. The jobseeker is at the mercy of the employer and senses that he or she needs to impress the interviewer. As a result, jobseekers are nervous, unsure of themselves, and tense up.

They shouldn't.

The power imbalance is a feeling and illusion. You are not at the mercy of the hiring process as a job seeker. This is an exchange between two adults. You are exchanging your skills, talent, time, and labor for the employer's money, insurance, and reasonable working conditions.

Sometimes the power balance tips towards the candidate. This depends on the job market conditions and for the role you are applying for. If an employer has had difficulty filling an opening, they will be under pressure to find a quality candidate and will be ready to throw everything but the kitchen sink at the right person.

In fact, the hiring manager is likely more nervous than you are because making a bad hire is costly and painful. A candidate can just walk away from a bad job, but a bad hire can cost a company majorly. For example, The U.S. Department of Labor estimates the cost of a bad hire to be around 30% of the employee's first-year earnings.

What is the point? You are a qualified candidate who brings high value to the job. If Mindset was all about self-belief and Discovery was about self-awareness, then Rebrand is about self-acceptance, then Interview is all about self-assurance.

As a career-changing pastor, you will have to shift your mindset. You need to shake imposter syndrome and believe that you do have talents, skills and abilities that have prepared you for your next role. Working in any ministry context requires a special person. Even if you never had the ministry of your dreams, you still picked up abilities that companies not only want, but need and will pay for.

When you walk into a job interview, you should never walk in with the mindset that you are desperate for a job and the company you are interviewing is dangling a role above you like a carrot. Walk into an interview with a mentality that says, "Hey company! You have something I want—the next step in my career. I have something that you want, time, talent, and abilities. Let's sit down as adults and discuss if this is a good fit. . . for both of us."

FRAME YOUR RESPONSES LIKE A STAR

If the first hurdle is the mindset, the second hurdle is the framing. How do you position your non-traditional experience in a way that makes sense to a hiring manager who may not even know what a pastor does? This is why I love the STAR Technique.

In the early part of my ministry journey, I sensed a call to plant a church in New York City. Part of that journey was to undergo a two-day assessment with a major denomination to test my aptitude to take on such a massive challenge. It was the most stressful job interview of my life.

The night before the first day, a friend who had gone through a similar assessment in another city told me, "Eric, don't overthink it. They just want to see if they like you."

Now, I think my friend was only partially right. They wanted to hear my story, my vision, my plan, all the way down to how I would build a team, create relational inroads into the community, and (of course) raise money. Yet there was also lots of time baked into the agenda to get to know me during fellowship, meals, breakout sessions, and conversations. Then I realized, this is kind of like a church job interview. . . on steroids.

This is why the STAR method matters to you as a job seeker looking to transition from the church to the marketplace. How you demonstrate your value in a job interview situation is different than in a church job interview—where you are conditioned to just try to be liked.

In the marketplace, the people who hire want to like you as a candidate, but they also want to know what value that you bring to the organization. Essentially, you are an asset to the team that they are paying lots of money for on a regular basis. Therefore, they expect a level of performance. I am not saying this to scare you, but to prepare you. Being well liked is not enough.

In short, STAR stands for Situation, Task, Action, Result.

Imagine that you're applying for a Project Manager job and the interviewer asks, "Share a time in your career where you managed a large project with multiple stakeholders."

You can answer:

- Situation: "Every year, our church operated a large week-long program for children in the community to have fun, play games, and learn."

- Task: "This program required 50+ volunteers, all of whom had to be vetted, trained, and placed into different functions for the event, including a variety of responsibilities based on their skill level and qualifications."

- Action: "I had to recruit these volunteers, run all background checks, interview them to understand their skills, and place them in the right roles so they could flourish. I also ran monthly training sessions for the four months leading up to the event."

- Result: "As a result, each year we welcomed over 200 kids to the program that week, and we were able to serve our community in a massive way. This helped us build our reputation in the city as a trusted faith institution that cares about children and families."

With this answer, you demonstrated to the interviewer that you are a strong leader that is organized in recruitment, training, staffing, and compliance. You showed that you are detail-oriented and can handle the massive responsibility of caring for children.

You can interview candidates and assess for skills. You are engaged in your community and have strong values. You know how to manage a large team and have the commitment and dedication to see projects through to completion. I would hire you.

Yet some ministers would sink themselves in a job interview simply because they do not know how to respond to that question.

WHEN TO NEGOTIATE SALARY (AND EVERYTHING ELSE)

Some time ago, I was coaching a seasoned pastor named Tim. Tim had unfortunately received some raw deals at churches where he had served. Though he was a dynamic leader, he struggled with deep insecurity about his likelihood of being hired, especially because of his age. He was in his late fifties when I met him. He would apply for roles, but often get rejected within a few days. Whenever he snagged an interview, he would not show the confidence necessary to be moved along in the process.

He had an interview for a great role at a regional bank where he would lead their Corporate Social Responsibility division, overseeing activities like volunteerism, nonprofit partnerships, and community collaboration. He was thrilled, and had his initial 30-minute interview with the Director of HR.

He called me right after the interview and told me it went great. He gave me a play-by-play of how the conversation went. I listened intently and was thrilled to hear the excitement in Tim's voice. But as he told me about the last few minutes of the conversation, my heart sank. Tim blew it because he didn't know when to negotiate.

At the end of the initial 30-minute interview, the Director of HR asked Tim if he had any questions. This interview was in October, and Tim's first question was "I know this role requires weekend work, and my daughter is graduating college the weekend of May 10th. Am I going to be able to get that off?"

I cringe just thinking about that, and I am sure the Director of HR did too. This was not Tim's fault. In traditional church interviews, this would be a totally normal request. But in the marketplace, these are the sort of things you ask later when you have leverage. Here's a simple template to understand corporate hiring processes to know how and when to ask questions.

Interview 1: The Phone Screen: Most companies are not going to put candidates in front of managers and team members until they have done some sort of screening to weed out poorly fitted candidates. This short interview, typically done over the phone or video call, is typically handled by somebody in the HR department to ask some basic questions about your skills, qualifications, and background.

This first interview is light touch and low leverage. The goal is to confirm you are a good fit for this role based on your qualifications. Do not overthink this first conversation. In most cases, this is just a formality and gatekeeping.

Some example questions they may ask:

- "Tell me about yourself."
- "What interested you in this job?"

They may also share their timeline to hire. Typically, this person is not too close to the manager or the team, so this is not the time to ask nitty gritty questions. It is simply to check alignment for their needs and yours.

You are simply there to find out what the role entails and ask basic questions. For example:

- "What is the hiring process for this role?"
- "What is the expected salary?"
- "When would you like a person in this role?"

This is not the time to ask about paid time off, whether the company does casual Fridays, if you will be getting a company credit card, or if you can take off for your daughter's graduation in 8 months. Save that for later.

Interview 2: Meet Your Manager: Typically, if you pass the phone screen, you will next meet the person who would be your boss. This person is called the hiring manager. Depending on the role, this could happen in person or on Zoom. The interview typically lasts forty-five minutes to an hour. While the first interview with HR was about skills and qualifications, this will be more about culture and compatibility. Your potential future boss will be wondering, "Is this a person I want to work closely with every day?" You should be asking yourself the same question.

This interview is high touch and medium leverage. The goal of this interview is to confirm you're a good fit for this role based on a culture match.

Some example questions they may ask:

- "Tell me about a time you overcame a challenge at work."

- "How would you coworkers describe your communication style?"

- "If you were a dinosaur, what kind would you be?" (You know, normal questions like that.)

You as a job seeker need to understand yourself, your working style, and your preferences. For example, I enjoy working more on my own than with others. I am naturally introverted, and though I can be collaborative, I prefer to be on my own thinking, dreaming, writing, designing, and being creative. If I were applying for a sales role where the expectation was to make 200 phone calls a day to prospects, I would die. Knowing how, when, and where you do your best work is critical to explain in an interview.

Interview 3 (if applicable): Meet Your Team: Not every company will do this, and some do even more than three interviews, but in general, if you make it this far then you are one of the finalists who made it past HR and the big boss. If this were a video game, you are now in Bowser's final castle.

Sometimes the third interview is a presentation, or just a meet-and-greet with potential future teammates. The level of seriousness varies vastly. I have been in panel interviews where it felt like a formality, and the mentality seemed to be "this person is a shoo-in; we just want one last checkpoint." I also went through a five round interview process as a candidate where I had to present a 45-minute workshop to four people for my final round, and after that I did not get the offer.

If the first interview with HR was about skills and qualifications, and the second interview with the hiring manager was more about culture and compatibility, then the third is about energy and vibe. I know not many books like this will say it, but it's the unsaid reality of that final round of interviews. If your potential future coworkers don't connect well with you here, your likelihood of getting the offer is extremely low. Typically, there are 2–3 candidates at this point, and they're going to pick the one they enjoy being with the most. Every company culture and hiring process is different, but this is a common model.

The questions may be like the manager's questions, but anticipate questions like these:

- "How do you solve problems?"
- "What is your philosophy on. . ." a certain element of the job.
- I was once in a panel interview and someone asked me, "so since you grew up in Pennsylvania, but you live in New York, where is your sports allegiance?" When I told him that I like the Yankees and the Steelers, I made some fans (and enemies) with my future coworkers.

This interview is medium touch and high leverage. The goal is to show your future colleagues that you can bring the right energy, that you are easy to get along with, and that you will be a great addition to the team. The manager already thinks that—you won him or her over already—but now you must win over a whole group of people. But you're a pastor, this part should be easy. Just have fun!

HOW TO NEGOTIATE SALARY

Now you are wondering, when do I negotiate salary, PTO, hybrid versus in-office, and all those important details that make me nervous? Only after you've received an offer. Once the company has gone through all the work, energy, and manpower to get to the point of extending an offer, then you hold all the leverage. I am not saying that if they offer you $50,000, that you can come back requesting $100,000. I am saying that this is the time to make your asks, whatever they are. Here is how to talk salary.

I had a pastor call me because he was offered $65,000 a year for his first job after full-time ministry. As a father of two living in New York City, he wanted to negotiate for a little more, which was outside his cultural and religious norm.

After a few minutes of talking, I told him to call back the hiring manager and use this simple script. Remember that calling is important. This cannot be done via e-mail.

"Thank you so much for this offer. I'm so excited for this opportunity. I did some research on Glassdoor, Zip Recruiter, and Indeed and saw that this title in New York City earns closer to $70K–$80K. I believe that my unique background as someone who has spent years working in training, leadership and program development means that I bring an above average skill set with me to this role. I want to counter your offer of $65K with $70K. Is there room in the budget for this bump? If so, I'm comfortable signing on right away."

Then wait. (This is the hard part).

This pastor texted me later and told me that he did it! He almost puked, but he did it! 3 hours later he texted me: "70K!!!!!"

I was so happy for him, and celebrated that win, but felt a slight tinge of regret. Should he have asked for $75K? They probably would have done it. They really liked him, and as of this writing, he still works there 2 years later.

How do you negotiate for more money?

Let's call it out. You think it's icky, gross, and un-spiritual. I get it.

You can pass a bucket every week or send your wife to work every day while you write sermons in Panera Bread with those unlimited free spritzers but asking for a few extra thousand dollars from a company with millions of dollars is gross. I know, we all believe weird things. I used to think I wouldn't get back hair as an adult like my dad, but here we are.

Unfortunately, it is not as easy as barging into your boss' office or your next board meeting, and slamming your fist on the desk and yelling, "Show me the money!"

Talking about money and asking for more money should not only be a skill you should practice. Doing so can pay huge dividends in the long term.

Let's take the pastor above. He just got $5,000 more per year. That's one more big family vacation, one or two months of rent in New York, or one hot dog at Yankees Stadium.

But even more than that, as he gets promoted, and receives merit and cost of living increases, it compounds on his initial compensation. That $5,000 will keep growing and growing. Not asking for a pay raise is costing you even more than you think.

Here is a three-step process to negotiate for more money at your current job or a future job. Remember, the best time to negotiate is after an offer is extended. Do not ask for more money after the first interview. You have less leverage then.

Don't just say, "I want to be promoted and a comparable pay raise of X." Instead say, "I want to grow as a professional, and one way to do that is that I want to be involved in strategic and high value projects within the organization. What are some areas that need attention that you think I should focus on?"

What did you just do? You didn't walk into the boss' office demanding a handout. You walked in with your hand extended. You communicated that you want to be helpful and take on more responsibilities in the organization. You're making everyone's life easier, and not being a greedy jerk. Nice work. I knew your mother -in-law was wrong about you.

There are two approaches here. One approach is to ask the one who holds the purse strings what problems they want solved. That's fine. The other approach is to bring a problem that you want to solve. I think that is better. The big difference is that you're walking in with a value proposition, and a bargaining chip to negotiate a raise.

Ok, but what does that have to do with pay? Everything. You may or may not get there in that initial conversation, but let's imagine that you take on new projects and initiatives, managing staff, streamlining processes, or creating more value. You can continue the conversation with this simple segue.

Don't imply that "I am overworked and not being paid enough." Instead say, "Let's suppose I take on this new project. This is going to be a lot of hours for me and bring tremendous value to the organization in these critical areas. It would only be fair if I were compensated more for this additional work. Would it be crazy if we could arrange where if I take on this additional load, I could be paid X% more annually?"

It could be broken down in different ways depending on your industry, but let's imagine this in the church world for a minute.

Suppose you are an underpaid youth pastor who eats Ramen noodles and still has Windows 95. (I've been there, keep fighting the good fight.) In my youth pastor days, I once tried walking into the board meeting to ask for a raise, and I got nowhere. Do you know why? Because I had no reason to be given a raise. I had been doing the same amount of work for the same amount of money for years, why did I need a raise?

My reasons for just wanting more money were not particularly compelling either. I told them that I had student loan debt and needed to replace my vehicle. That did not move them to want to throw a few extra grand into my paycheck every year.

Look at it from their angle. Did they have any guarantee that I would increase my workload with more money? No. Would you be willing to give me a raise? Me neither.

But what if I came in and said, "Hey I have been the Youth Pastor here for 2 years and I want to grow in my skills as a ministry professional. I noticed that Ms. Suzy, the 79-year-old volunteer kids director is starting to get a bit overwhelmed with our growing kids ministry. What would your thoughts be if I worked on a transition plan to help Ms. Suzy and took over the scheduling, staffing, background checks, and supply orders for our kid's ministry? Do you think that could be valuable?"

Now suddenly, the board is intrigued. That would be helpful for our kid's ministry, what a team player! This young pastor is going places! He may even become a real pastor one day! (That is a joke to make sure you are paying attention.)

But of course, I am going to ask for more money. Why? Because more value means more money.

Don't say, "I'm working hard, and things are great." Instead say, "Here is a list of everything that I have done in my functional job (things that are on my job description). Here is a list of the things that I have done above and beyond my functional role, and here are the areas I want to grow in moving forward."

Here's the dark and dirty secret. No one is going to advocate for you to get a pay raise. No one. Unless you "have your receipts" on why you deserve a raise, it won't happen.

Finally, it's standard to ask for more money before accepting a job. It's totally expected that you will ask for more money after the initial offer is made. You work for money; you don't have to act like you do not. If you are bringing value, that value should be rewarded. If it's not, find somewhere else where it will be.

If the salary is not negotiable, you can negotiate other aspects of the offer. I have seen professionals negotiate an extra week of PTO, or a change in title (from Manager to Director or Director to Vice President), some have negotiated a three-days-per-week -in-the-office schedule down to two days. The opportunities are endless.

BUILDING CONFIDENCE WITH INFORMATIONAL INTERVIEWS

This is great but now what? As shared in chapter 3, networking is the name of the game for all jobseekers but doubly so for career changers like you. The best way to build (or in most cases rebuild) your confidence is with practice. This is not looking in front of the mirror and talking to yourself, though that does help. This is human to human contact, eyeball to eyeball. You must learn to dial in your elevator pitch, how to present what you bring to the table, and how to frame your ministry experience in a way that makes sense to the person listening.

If you need practice in this area (and we all do), I suggest you begin scheduling informational interviews. For those unfamiliar with this term, this is when you schedule time with somebody working a job or in an industry that is interesting to you and ask them for 15–30 minutes to learn more about their career journey and story.

This is not time to "buy you coffee and pick your brain." Most professionals are busy, and especially if you are a stranger, they don't want to spend an hour having coffee with you. I know this may be surprising to hear, but not everyone wants to have coffee with you. (Did I mention that job seeking is humbling?)

A simple way to get time on someone's calendar in a nutshell is identify a common denominator, share your reason for meeting, and just ask.

If I get a LinkedIn message from someone that says, "Hi Eric, I saw you went to Liberty, so did I. Want to connect?", I ignore it. It found a common denominator and it asked for time, but this sounds like you are going to sell me Tupperware or Avon. Hard pass.

If the message says, "Hi Eric, I want to apply for a role at your company, want to connect?", I am ignoring it. You framed why you wanted to meet, and you asked, but these reeks of a pray-and-spray networking where you are sending the same canned message to every person at the company hoping that some sucker bites.

Watch the magic when you combine all three:

"Hi Eric, I saw you graduated from Liberty University, so did I, class of 2012. I also see we have a mutual connection through Joey Reed. His brother Ethan and I were in the same dorm. Anyways, I am reaching out because I saw a Project Manager role at your company, and I wanted to learn more about the position. Would you be open to a 15–30-minute Zoom call where I can learn more about the company and your experience there? Let me know if you have a good time and I can send you a link."

I would reply to this.

Also, did you notice that this person did not say, "I am free tomorrow at 2 p.m., and Friday at 9 a.m." The person you want to book time with is doing you a favor by spending time with you. Work around their schedule, even if it's slightly inconvenient for you. I once met a pastor for coffee at 6 a.m. on a weekday because I wanted to learn from him, and that is when he did meetings. I have had many coffee meetings with pastors in my career, and this one was incredibly life-giving, but I had to work around his schedule.

This type of message is personable and shows thought and care. This is how you earn an informational interview. Now I may or may not be hiring for the Project Manager role, I may or may not know the manager or the team or any of that, but I work in the company, and I am an "inside connection."

Remember the referral bonuses from Chapter 3? This is why people are eager to spend a few minutes getting to know interested candidates. It may take me 30 minutes to meet you, hear your story and confirm you are not crazy. But for most people, that is all it takes to refer someone. Nobody wants to waste their time referring a dud, so do not be a dud.

Once you are on the video call, do not waste time talking about news, sports, or weather. Remember this person is a professional giving their time to you. Have four or five pointed questions prepared and be sure to take notes.

Here are some sample questions:

- How did you end up working at this company, and what do you enjoy about it?

- What are some of the biggest challenges that you can share about the business that you think this role I am going to apply for can solve?

- What advice do you wish someone would have given you in the interview process?

- (Most important) Are you willing to provide a referral to me for this role?

Do not hang up on this call until you ask for a referral. The way referrals work varies vastly based on the size and complexity of the company, but you want to get clear on the call how to do it so you can position yourself well for the next step.

One important note here is that referrals are great, but finding an advocate is even better. A referral is somebody who will push your resume through their system to get exposure to you faster. This is a light amount of work and responsibility. However, an advocate goes one step further. Perhaps they reach out directly to the hiring manager and hype you up, or they follow up with the recruiter to ensure that you get an interview.

The only way you can turn a referral into an advocate is by keeping the relationship warm. Nobody likes to feel as though they were used for a referral and never spoken to again so a few ways you can keep that relationship warm is by sending a small gift after they refer you—even a $10 Starbucks gift card is great. You can comment on their posts on LinkedIn and share them with your network. Once you start interviewing, keep them abreast of what is happening and be sure to always show gratitude.

The more senior a person is within the organization, the more likely their view of you as a candidate will be favorable. I am not saying this is fair or equitable, but if the president of the company tells a manager that you are a fantastic fit for this role, that holds much more weight than an entry level person. It just does.

Here is the template to snag informational interviews.

- Write a thoughtful note via LinkedIn messaging, or through e-mail with an e-mail lookup tool (there are multiple online).

- Prepare questions to ask. The four questions on the previous page work, and ideally you want at least one question pertaining to the role itself to show that you did your homework.

- Ask for the referral on the call to begin begin the application process.

- Turn your referral into an advocate by keeping the relationship warm.

I would say that if you are a jobseeker, and especially as a career changer, you should be spending most of your time in informational interviews. Not fine-tuning your resume or applying to any job that looks interesting, but pavement pounding, meeting people, and building professional relationships.

Not only does this propel your job search, but it helps you grow your humble confidence—the most important skill you need in the job search.

THE PRINCIPLE OF HUMBLE CONFIDENCE

Church interviews and marketplace interviews could not be more different. Those differences hinge largely on one element—how the candidate presents him or herself in the interview. This is why so many pastors face such a massive hurdle when it comes to the interview, and why I dedicate a whole chapter of this book to it.

For starters, church interviews are weird. I interviewed for an associate pastor role one time where every elder, deacon, and their spouse attended. My wife and I received rapid-fire questions for 2 hours from over 20 people for a $35,000-a-year job. A bit overkill in my view, but water under the bridge at this point. At least we got a free lunch out of the deal.

Church interview questions will ask you about your enneagram number, why you named your kids their names (or why you don't have kids yet), and what your biggest sin is. That last part is real. In my view, church interviews are very weird, tense, and awkward. I think every seminary degree should include a course on HR but that is a different book.

Companies tend to be a bit smarter about their interview process, mostly because they are bringing in a larger volume of new hires and want to avoid getting sued. Imagine that!

Many pastors bomb marketplace interviews because they treat them like church interviews. They fall into the same weird, tense and awkward patterns that they are used to. Here are five of the most common pitfalls to avoid when interviewing for a marketplace role as someone with a ministry background

- They complain about previous jobs. Complaining about a previous job is just bad practice in general. It is like going on a first date where the other person drones on and on about how much their ex broke their heart. This is a job interview, not a Taylor Swift concert. Hearing someone complain about how awful their church job (or any job) will just come across as a bad look in general. Keep your answers focused on why you are the best candidate for the role. Be future-focused and save your trauma and drama for your therapist.

  Best practice: When asked about why you want to leave your work in the church, simply respond with this, "I have loved my time working in the local church and want to expand myself to this role to face new challenges and opportunities such as. . ." This is way better than complaining. Just don't complain.

- They bring up their home life. I know some of you are going to fall out of your seat because your family is such a massive part of church interviews. But your marital status, ages and names of your kids should be discussed after you are hired. I know you love your family, but they're hiring you for the skills you bring to the table, not that you are a "family man" or "family woman."

  Best practice: Because of employment law, it's very unlikely they'll even ask about life outside of work. That's fine. There is no reason to give more information than they need that could color the way the interviewer views your candidacy. Stick to the facts, and do not bring up your kids or family unless the person interviewing you does first.

- They give "church-y" answers—or don't reframe them. I get where this is tricky, especially for those of us who have spent our careers in the church. You're selling transferable skills, not how you're the world's best pastor (which I am sure you are). For example, if you are asked about a challenge that you overcame professionally, instead of sharing about how the worship leader quit on Good Friday, and you had to scramble to find a replacement because Easter is the Super Bowl of Churches (do people still say that? No one I know!), share about interpersonal conflict you had with a board member, how you coached a volunteer who lacked direction, or how you fundraised for a giving campaign. That makes sense to the interviewer. Comparing the holiest day in the church calendar to a football game doesn't.

Best Practice: Have 3–4 stories internalized for behavioral or situational questions like this one. Write them down on a sticky note and put them where you can see them (if interviewing on a video call).

- They feel like an imposter, and act like one. I totally get that for those of us changing industries it is near impossible not to feel like a massive imposter. You feel like that high school kid walking into Wendy's for your first "real job." Before you gave one last sad and scared glance at your mom waving you on from her minivan, you took a deep breath and told yourself, "I got this." You are going to be nervous, that is normal. However, interviews are a chance to show off, not downplay or minimize your achievements.

Best practice: Remember, the people interviewing you are not going to waste their time if they do not think you are a viable candidate. They're already impressed with you and know that you qualify. At this point, it's just helping them see you're the best fit for the role.

- They rely on their charisma, not their competency. Companies want to hire people they trust, and they trust people that are both warm and competent. We as pastors have no problem being friendly, gregarious, and likable, but when it comes to jumping into a whole new domain of work, we fumble and stumble. Do not fall into the trap of thinking that your charisma will be your only weapon to win over someone in an interview. Be prepared to have robust, well-thought-out answers. In short, know what you are talking about.

Best Practice: There is no excuse to not know the details of a company before an interview. The company most likely has the following: a website, LinkedIn, social media, earnings calls, Glassdoor.com. It's all out in the open. Do the hard work to be prepared on the day of the interview.

What is humble confidence?

In church interviews, decision makers typically value modesty, likeability and "fit." Those things matter in marketplace interviews as well yet in a marketplace interview, the question that is under the surface is, "How much of a risk is bringing this person onto the team?"

Hiring is at its core about finding a person who can get the job done. It is not about who is the nicest, funniest, or has the most dazzling personality. It is about "can this person execute the duties of the job with the minimum amount of risk?"

You must have confidence that your skills and abilities as a pastor translate into the needs of the company and do everything you can to message that to the person interviewing you. That is it. Do not overcomplicate it. You do not want to come across as a cocky, know-it-all and you don't want to come across as a lost puppy that is just looking for a home.

You want to eliminate risk in the mind of the person interviewing you and use that conversation as an opportunity to display how you are the best fit for the job. Remember, interviews are two -way streets and just as they have the job, you have the skills. When you approach it as two professionals exchanging talent for money, you will begin getting more interviews and ultimately a fantastic offer.

YOUR NEXT STEPS

1. Do you have the self-assurance that you are a high-quality candidate who brings value to the jobs that you are interviewing for? If not, why not? If so, how can you present that when speaking with decision makers?

2. What are some of the common interview questions you will be asked based on the roles that I am applying for? How can you frame your experiences in the STAR technique to ensure they make sense to those interviewing you?

3. What common pitfalls are you prone to in interviews that you need to begin correcting now? If you are unsure of the most common mistakes pastors make in job interviews, download my free PDF at ihelppastorsgetjobs.com.

Chapter 5: Sustainability

"If your life is so full that you can't have a cup of tea with a friend,
wander through a park on a sunny afternoon or read through a non-
fiction book before bed, you may be maximizing the hours but you're
wasting the years."

—AUTHOR UNKNOWN

"You are at your pastoral best when you go unnoticed."

—EUGENE PETERSON

A NEW REALITY

THERE IS THIS UNFORTUNATE image that some people on the internet have of me and my view of pastoral ministry and the local
church. I've been accused by strangers on the internet as someone
who "dunks on churches" and "wounds pastors" and "has a goal to
get pastors out of ministry."

None of that is true. I love the local church, and I love serving her in whatever capacity God calls me to. In this book, I am
proposing a new reality. A Market Street Pastor is just a pastor

who also works another job. His or her ministry is not just in the church, but in the marketplace. All of their life is a ministry.

Despite everything I went through in ministry that I shared at the start of this book—an unjust termination, an NDA, and near homelessness—I returned to pastoral ministry three years later as a church planter being sent by a local church and mentored by a godly pastor.

In 2016, I planted All Saints Church in The Bronx, a community in New York City. The work was completely pioneered, with no major outside funding and no "parachute" team coming in from the outside. I was able to build slowly, and God brought the people and resources to make it work.

I led that congregation for seven years, we baptized adults, dedicated babies, prayed for the dying, and performed funerals. We partnered with local schools, parks, and community organizations to make our community better. We endured the COVID-19 pandemic even though we were unable to meet in person for 20 months. We helped plant two new churches led by local covocational leaders.

God did a mighty work in and through me and I Help Pastors Get Jobs and this book is the culmination of that season of ministry.

In 2022, as church plants like mine were closing left and right around the city and nation, a mentor of mine called me and told me something that has stuck with me for years. He said, "Eric, you never had the biggest church (I didn't), you never had the most money (I most certainly didn't) but here we are two years into Covid and All Saints is still standing. . ." It was. That part was true.

He continued, "I think a large part of it has to do with the covocational model." He went on to explain in his work coaching and training church planters, his organization was getting calls every other week about planters who were shutting down shop and fleeing the city. He said the overwhelming reason was finances. They just couldn't afford to keep living here. He thought that my ministry could help, "Maybe you could start a ministry helping pastors make the switch from full time, salaried pastors to covocational ministers. . . especially around helping them get jobs."

And that is how this ministry was born.

The beautiful thing about covocational ministry is your salary is no longer tied to the money coming in through the tithes and offerings. If a wealthy family leaves, or an unexpected cost arises, you do not need to hit the panic button. I remember a service while I was pastoring where our executive pastor was on vacation, and I forgot to announce that we do an offering. When somebody asked me how to give digitally, I could not remember the Cashapp tag. I am not sure if we should call that bad business practice or fantastic kingdom practice.

Some may look at a covocational model of ministry as restrictive. It is if not done correctly. There are only so many hours in a day; are you not shortchanging your ministry if you go out and get a job? This is the chapter in the book most will gloss over, and no one should because if you do everything else in this book and then keep attempting to pastor like you have been as a full timer, you will crash and burn within 6 months. I can guarantee it.

MIGUEL'S STORY

Miguel was one of my favorite pastors that I ever worked with because he had done the impossible in church planting. He launched a congregation in a large city in the northeast of the United States, and over the course of five years, the church had over 800 worshippers coming. The congregation that he led had a multimillion budget, large staff, and had just wrapped up a capital campaign to buy a historic church in the community and renovate it for their permanent home.

If you know nothing about church planting, Miguel is a unicorn. Yet Miguel felt this strange tension in his soul which he could not quite get his finger on until he went to a denominational conference on the other side of the country where everything changed. At the conference, he decided to have dinner with some seminary buddies the night after the last session. They went to a local restaurant, ordered dinner, and began sharing their ministry stories about how God had been working in and through them since they walked across that stage a few years back to receive their seminary degrees.

Miguel was used to the typical pastor talk that happens at conferences like these. How many are you running? How many does your building seat? Why can't anyone volunteer in the nursery? The usual topics. However, this group was different. They had deep trust and admiration for one another, and Miguel knew it would not be a business-as-usual talk. One pastor broke the ice, I got into ministry because my dad did. He pastored an 80-person church and knew everyone. He cared for people in their most vulnerable moments and walked them through every season you could imagine. I am leading a church of 500 now and am basically just a CEO. I don't walk with people; I manage programs and projects and put out fires.

The next guy spoke up sharing similar frustrations. How he simply felt like he's feeding into the consumeristic sensibilities of American evangelicalism. He shared how most of the time he simply felt like a politician, pandering to the congregation on whatever hot button topic that they care about that month. He said he felt lost, but could not push the eject button because he needed to feed his family.

The third guy shared how his marriage was in trouble. His wife was frustrated with the low pay and earning potential in pastoral ministry, and even though they were making it, they were not saving anything for the future and certainly not thriving. He loved his church and wanted to stay in ministry but did not know if his wife would tolerate it. Her resentment was growing.

Finally, it was Miguel's turn. He admitted, "I am the poster boy for our denomination in terms of church planting. We have one of the fastest growing churches in our network. I am asked to speak to pastors on how to grow their churches, but the truth is, I am a phony. Of the hundreds of people who come to our church, only about 5% of them are new converts—the rest are transfer growth who came to us because we offered a better product than the other guys in town."

Miguel realized in that conversation that his issue was that he got into church planting to reach people far from God. He was—about 50 people in total were completely unchurched or de -churched—and his church plant was their first time in church in years or ever. He wished he could just lead a church with those 50 people, but felt like he couldn't because his salary, brand, and image were tied to the success of his congregation.

Miguel went home and told his wife he wanted to quit and become a marketplace missionary, serving the urban poor while working a job and training others how to live on mission. His wife said, "let's pray about it," and after a few months of discernment and counsel, they decided it was best for the family. A few months later, Miguel created a succession plan and transitioned from lead pastor into a marketplace role. Now he trains others how to make disciples, including some large church pastors. Imagine that.

People thought he was crazy, but he now has a strong sense of confidence in what God is calling him to do. Importantly, he can do it because he chose a new reality.

WHAT IS THE POINT?

The point of this whole book is to be a Market Street Pastor. Someone who works hard, is paid well, can be active in their community and equip their church for ministry. This is a model for sustainable ministry in the 21st century and beyond.

I often get asked, "Well, when I know it's time to leave my current ministry context for what God may have for me next?" My answer is always the same, when you have something to run to, not something to run from.

Challenges in ministry will always be present. Disgruntled deacons, building projects that fall apart, staff who quit, members who lie, toilets that overflow. That is not a reason to jump ship. The reason you jump ship is when you see land, and you plunge down knowing that you can swim.

One of the greatest indicators that a person is not ready to transition in their ministry journey is when they are not having honest conversations with those closest to them about their intentions. I do not think God honors our secrecy. I understand some situations can be stickier than others, but if you are going to make this move, you need people in your corner who can be your advocate—starting with your spouse. I am surprised I have to type this, but I have met some pastors who have told me more about their ideas to transition in ministry than they have told their own spouses. This behavior reeks of dysfunction.

After you get intentional and realistic about where you want to go and what you want to do, you now need to begin re-prioritizing how you spend your time, energy and giftings. The three-columns system can help.

THE THREE-COLUMNS SYSTEM

When I was leading All Saints Church, we were by no means a large church. In fact, by some standards, we were more like a glorified small group. Yet, at our peak we had five paid staff in our regular sized church. I was paid part-time, and so was our Executive Pastor . We had a Virtual Assistant who functioned as a bookkeeper, and our Kids Director and Worship Director were on contracts.

Everybody had another job outside of All Saints, but we were able to have a solid paid staff and robust volunteer force that made our church operate for as long as it did. This started when I took an audit of my time and energy as a pastor and thought carefully about three things: What can I do, what can I delegate to someone else, and what is happening that does not need to?

I took out a sheet of paper, made three columns: "can do," "give away," and "eliminate." I categorized every single activity that happened in the church each year.

Done properly, this list will humble you rather quickly, because you will realize how much you are doing that could be delegated or eliminated.

When I did this exercise, I realized I only had 2 jobs that only I could do, and they were:

- Set the vision & direction of the church with input and collaboration from others.

- Manage the preaching calendar and ensure each preaching slot was filled for the year.

Even in both of those, my work was shared with other staff and lay leaders. It was incredibly humbling, because I spent years in a full-time vocational ministry role. Although I busied myself with plenty of activity, what was moving the mission forward always felt elusive. Honestly, I always felt tired.

I am ashamed to say that there was a time in my ministry when I thought being a pastor meant being the guy on the stage holding the microphone with all eyes on him. I realize now what a fool I was, because my job description all along was to equip the saints to do the work of the ministry, not to do the work of the ministry myself.

There was also a time in ministry when I felt this undue burden that I needed to do everything since I was the "paid professional." I wonder how many other pastors are stifling the growth of their members by similar mindsets.

ACTIVATING LEADERS AND LIVING ON MISSION

I anticipate I sound like a broken record but for this point, I do not mind. To attempt to engage in covocational ministry while doing "business as usual" is a fast track to burnout, frustration, and ultimately giving up. You and I have been conditioned by the systems in our religious institutions that pastors are not only super Christians but superheroes. Those of you who are pastors and reading this book know that neither of these things are true.

I don't believe that it's right for a pastor to revamp their priorities until they have a clear understanding of where they are going and what they are doing. In the same way, I advise against moving forward with anything in this book until you have an honest conversation with those in your inner ministry circle about a plan. This could be your board, leadership team, or church council but you cannot attempt this alone.

A template that I would suggest leading with is basic. Just like you learned elevator pitches:

- Where you are from.

- A moment of change.

- Where are you going?

  This is that with a slight bend:

- How we have done things.

- How things are changing.

- Where you can plug in and support.

There's a cliché saying in ministry settings, particularly fundraising, but it holds true. People do not give to need; they give to vision. The same can be true as you frame these conversations. You can approach it with an attitude of "giving up" or an attitude of "leveling up"—which type of leader would you want to follow?

For those who want to get granular, here's a script you can share:

"Over the last several years, we have had a ministry model where I as the pastor have carried most of the weight of ministry. This includes preaching, leading Sunday School, discipling new believers, baptisms, weddings, funerals, hospital visits, fielding angry emails, and occasionally shoveling the sidewalk after a snowstorm. I realized that I was not living out my true calling as a pastor which is to work with others in building God's kingdom, and I sense He wants to change how we do things around here. For the past several years you have been a faithful attendee of our Sunday School class and I want to empower you to teach our adult Sunday School class. You and I will meet once a month to discuss the topics. I'd like you to share your ideas for the classes, and I'll provide feedback. We will pray together, and I will be your biggest champion and advocate in that ministry. What do you think?"

Some of you fell out of your seat just now, and are wondering, did this person even go to seminary? What will people think if I as the pastor don't teach Sunday School? Will the church hold an uprising in the foyer and vote me off the island?

Just try it. Even if you are highly risk averse, try it for two Sundays and go take a vacation. Try it with alternating Sundays for the summer. Give this volunteer a once-a-month slot and ramp up. Just try. But in the words of Red-Hot Chili Peppers, give it away, give it away, give it away now.

Imagine if you did this with five leaders, or ten, or twenty. What kind of church would you have when your investment is in leaders who are leading ministries? Then, another crazy idea (though not really): what if they started doing the same to others? New ministries could be launched, new churches could be planted, but most importantly, new disciples could be made.

Didn't Paul tell Timothy something like this? 2 Timothy 2:2 rings a bell.

YOUR NEXT STEP: JUST BE HONEST.

One of the unfortunate parts of my job is when the pastor calls me to find a marketplace job because he committed a moral sin that disqualified him from ministry. There are few phone calls more painful than listening to the hurt in a pastor's voice after he shipwrecks his marriage, his ministry, and reputation for a short-term pleasure.

I do not get into the weeds of the circumstances that led to his or her departure from ministry, that is not my main duty to pastors. I do find a curious and repeated theme: they just were not honest. They were not honest with their staff, their spouse, their God, or themselves. They were afraid to ask for help. They were too scared to shake the status quo. They were fearful of what would happen if they stepped out into what God had next for them, so in some cases, they blew it all up.

We as pastors are always positioned to be helpers, so we struggle to ask for help. I get it. Once I tried to move a bookshelf by putting one end on a desk chair and wheeling it across the parking lot at work. If you are honest with people, some will leave your church, others will ask or force you to leave. Some will judge you, say you couldn't quite hack it, and have every opinion you can imagine on why you chose this path—but let them.

Your goal is to work hard, provide for your family, be active in your community, and equip my church for ministry.

HOW DOES CHANGE HAPPEN?

Dr. John Kotter is a Harvard Business School Professor and wrote the book on Leading Change. He presents an eight-step process on how to manage change based on his research. Overlaying those principles with the change that you plan to make as a full-time pastor into a covocational pastor may be helpful:

Step 1: Create an Urgency. We have already touched on this a bit but are you suffering in silence because of your financial, moral or personal dilemma that brought you this far into the book? Your first step needs to be to be open and honest with the right people at the right time with the right information. If you have a highly pragmatic board, there is nothing wrong with just showing the numbers and sharing how this model of ministry is not sustainable and how it can be made better.

Step 2: Form a Coalition. Your Sunday School attendee-turned -leader could be the first person in your coalition, but you need people beyond you that see the vision, get the vision, and are willing to walk arm-and-arm with you to execute the vision, knowing that there will be detractors and naysayers along the way. Pastor, you need people to do this with, don't go this alone.

Step 3: Develop a Vision. This is critical since people follow vision and not need. Here's a "real talk" moment. No one wants to feel like they are on a sinking ship. If your communication is simply, "we're not able to fund this ministry," "we're not able to make disciples," or "I am burnt out and don't want to be here," you're not creating a compelling vision worth following. Make sure you're communicating this as what we are running to, not what we are running from.

Step 4: Communicate the Vision. To reiterate what was said in Step 3, now it is time to message this to the congregants. You must be wise and cautious about who gets what information when. For example, key leaders and volunteers should know about this change before Randy and Becki who only come on Easter but always have an opinion. I can't stand Randy and Becki and I know you can't either. Create a clear communication plan and execute it carefully.

Step 5: Remove obstacles. It is critical to have tight feedback loops with your leaders as you ask them to step into these new roles. This is not a moment to drop responsibility onto their lap and walk away mumbling under your breath, "call if you need me." I would advise a weekly or biweekly check-in during the early days to ensure they are being supported in what you are asking them to do. Remember, you are asking them to step up in a massive way, so step up to lead them in a similar way.

Step 6: Create short term wins. Since people are naturally reluctant to change, be sure to celebrate every small win. In a previous church, we had a mobile set up in a movie theater. One Sunday, the elevator broke. We were on the second floor. Four men from our church worked together to lift one of those heavy-duty plywood cases up two flights of stairs so we had sound for service. We snapped a photo and showed it the following Sunday to roaring applause. Teamwork in action. We celebrate every win.

Step 7: Consolidate wins. Continue to keep reiterating how this change is effective, what the church needs, and how you are in a better place as everyone pulls together to make a collective difference for the Gospel. Never stop thanking God for what He is doing.

Step 8: Anchor the change. When new people come, make sure it's embedded into the culture. This is how we do things as a church. It's a group effort, and we want everyone to be involved in the work of the ministry, not just the "professionals." People will come to your church with church baggage, and an expectation of how they think things should be done. Be OK with being different.

WHY DID YOU GET INTO MINISTRY?

As we conclude this book, I want to ask you to do some basement work. If you are unfamiliar with that expression, imagine that most of life is on the dance floor (sorry to the Baptists). This is work, kids, chores, family stuff, the place we spend most of our time.

However, sometimes we need to go onto the balcony and view the dance floor from a high level. We can't see everything when we are in it, sometimes we need to look from above and ask ourselves, "Is everything going as it should?" and "What can I tweak to make it even better?"

Balcony work is hard for pastors. That's why some of you have not done the three-column system exercise yet. To unplug yourself from the daily work to ask those thoughtful and introspective questions is not easy. It is why so few of us do it.

But it is even harder for most people than balcony work is basement work. This is when you don't look at outward activity of how you are spending your time, energy and resources but look inwardly. How am I doing, really? How is my soul, truly?

I shared five stories in this book of different pastors and the paths that led them to rethink their ministry vocation. These stories were not real people but amalgamates of hundreds of stories that I have heard in my work with I Help Pastors Get Jobs.

Where did you find yourself relating a little bit too much with the characters?

Was it the story of Bryan and Sheryl? The couple that realized if Bryan wanted to get a lead pastor role, they would have to leave the community they loved, where their kids were thriving and they didn't want to start over.

Maybe it was Ritchie's story. You are leading a small or developing congregation, and though you love the people and the ministry, you are continually frustrated and demoralized by low wages and earning potential.

Jack's story might have been your story. You live in a fishbowl and your family is suffering. You can see how challenging it is for the people you love the most, but you lack confidence to step out and try something different.

You may relate to Brianna's story. You know you can do something different, and have confidence in your skills and abilities, but the thought of being in a room with non-ministry people sharing your credentials strikes fear in your heart.

Or maybe you relate to Miguel. You are leading a robust and growing church but when you do your basement work, you realize this is not what you signed up for. You are not sure how to change.

If you can relate to any of these people, you are in good company. You are not the first person to struggle with the tension of ministry expectations that do not meet reality. You are not the first pastor who wondered, "Is this what God has called me to do?"

When you think about why you got into ministry, how would you respond?

For most of the Pastors that I speak with, the answer is the same: to preach God's word, care for God's people, and reach our community with the Gospel.

Let me ask a few follow-up questions:

- How much of your time and energy is spent doing that?
- Can you still do that without being full time in church ministry?
- Did the systems of religious institutions pull you from your first love and calling?

Sometimes the systems which man has created are what pull pastors from God's call.

When I was wrestling with my own transition in ministry, I decided to spend time with a wiser, older pastor that was part of my denomination. I visited his home in Connecticut, and we sat on his patio and drank some of the best sweet tea I have ever had.

I told him about my dream to plant and lead a church but said that I felt conflicted, as I also felt a call to the marketplace and was experiencing great success in my corporate job. He told me something that stayed with me for a long time. He said, "Jesus will build his church regardless of where you earn your income."

I realized that I had way too inflated a view of self, and way too small of a view of God. The guilt and shame that pastors feel when they sense they are abandoning the post that God has for them is often built within their own imaginations and perpetuated by institutions. We tell ourselves scripts like "the church will fall apart if I go part time," or "my people will never step up like I need them too." But Jesus said, "I will build my church." He did not say you would build his church, and He most certainly did not say "you build your church."

Have faith that He wants to redirect you into what He has next. It is not a lesser calling; it's a different calling.

WHAT IS A HEALTHY AND VIBRANT MINISTRY?

I want to end this book with an e-mail to bless and encourage you. This too can be your reality.

> Hey Eric,
>
> I want to thank you for what you do. We spoke a good while ago, and since then a lot has changed.
>
> My marriage is the best it has ever been. After we spoke and the big decision to leave ministry was before my family, my wife stepped up and (for the first time) expressed a sense of calling that she felt our family had to be a ministry family. That was a huge breakthrough for us. Though we were on this path before we even got

married, it has been a calling for me and not her. But when I was on the brink of leaving, she backed me up like never before.

Ministry work is not usually all that fun for me. But just a few days ago, my wife commented that for the first time in the years I've been doing this, she could see I was happy at work. And I realized she was right.

Since standing on the brink of burn out, my supporting church leaders have stepped up and helped me change the mindset of our church. We all work as a team and the expectations for me and everyone else are realistic. And as a result, the church body is more engaged and healthier.

Most weeks I'm still doubtful that this will be my life's work. We want kids, but struggle to even keep our home on our salaries; I still grapple with whether the physical and non-physical costs of working in ministry are worth my contribution to the kingdom (especially, when I know I could be effective as a top-tier volunteer, rather than staff); and most importantly, I wonder if I didn't have a better relationship and faith with God before being labeled a pastor.

Either way, I know I'm doing good work right now. I know my church loves me and supports me. And I'm proud of what we've accomplished this year, growing into a much stronger and healthier church. I have no doubt God could have accomplished this without me. But thanks to my wife's commitment to our calling and support for me, and some other great friends, I got to lead through this season.

However, you have also been a tremendous help. Your Twitter and emails have provoked thoughtful ideas for better church culture and practices. Ideas which I've had the privilege to actualize. The terms of my employment are appropriate and reasonable, and I have ensured that in my absence, the next pastor will be hired with reasonable expectations and qualifications.

It has also been a great help to know that with each passing day, week, month, and year, I am not wasting my chance to change careers. Career-wise, I'm still considerably young. I know that if I were to pursue a career change, it wouldn't be impossible. But that won't always be the case. Like you, I have an entrepreneur's mindset, and I'm always thinking through goals and strategy, and thus always thinking ahead. So, I am reminded every day that if I'm going to get out of ministry, my best path is to do it as soon as possible.

But because of IHPGJ, that pressure and stress doesn't haunt me like it [used] to. Right now, I'm in ministry, my family and church are doing okay, and I'm proud of the work I'm doing. And I can take my time to do good work for the church in my position, because I know that if the time comes for me to leave, no matter how many more months or years I put into this, when it's time to do the next thing, there is someone I can call to help me use all this growing experience in a new field.

So, thank you for giving me the courage to be a pastor while I'm in the prime of my working years. Thank you for the wisdom you share on the internet (a rare compliment). And thank you for unintentionally reinvigorating my marriage and calling.

Someday I'll probably reach out again offering you some cash for your services. Today, I just want to say thank you for being there for a stranger. You haven't increased your revenue because of me yet, but your work has helped me endure in ministry longer than I thought I could.

Thanks man,
Alex

CLOSING WORDS

I shared bits and pieces of my story throughout this book, and I suppose it's only fair that I share where I stand with the local church now. After my family transitioned from New York, we relocated to Pennsylvania and began attending a church outside of our tradition. After a few months, the pastor asked me if I would prayerfully step into serving the church as a lay leader.

The funny thing about the timing is that my final Sunday preaching at the church that I founded was in March 2023, and I asked God a simple prayer, "Lord, give me one year to attend a church, rest, receive and not do anything beyond that." I knew I was not out of the ministry game forever, but I knew I needed some breathing room to regroup and to figure out what was next.

The conversations with the pastor and leadership team about me taking on a leadership role began in March 2024. I know that there are pastors who transition from church ministry never to return to a church again, and I get it. Sadly, I think a major reason for that is because they never experienced a healthy church, including the one that they led.

This will be the first time in my ministry that my family chose the church we worshiped in and then I got involved in ministry and service later, not the other way around. This dynamic alone is a game changer. It was our faith community first. This is the type of life and ministry you can have when you step out and bet on yourself.

I am grateful that I made the tough decision to pursue a covocational path and even though it is not perfect, it is a sweet time of ministry that puts me squarely within my gifts for this season. I am still able to work outside of the church, be home for dinner with my kids, and have space for friendships, recreation, and joy. I am blessed and I want that for you as well. For the Lord and His Kingdom. Amen.

YOUR NEXT STEPS:

1. Have you ever faced a moment in your ministry where you realized the public image that your church or ministry has does not match the reality that is under the surface? How did you reconcile that?

2. Activating leaders to lead on mission is the most critical piece of this entire chapter. Do you have people in mind you can

begin having these honest conversations with about moving them into a more active leadership role?

3. As you do the basement work of remembering why you got into ministry, what did you come up with? What needs to be moved around and adjusted so that you can work on your giftings / callings?

Acknowledgements

To MY WIFE SARAH who believes in me more than I believe in myself, thank you for inspiring me. To my daughters, may you continue to grow into the women that God has wired you to become. To my family, thank you for your prayers and support to help me get my debut book off the ground.

Special shoutout to Mark Knight, my partner in I Help Pastors Get Jobs for helping me keep the central focus of serving the church and advancing the Kingdom. To Duncan Johnson, my editor who helped make a jumbled manuscript shine. I am grateful.

To All Saints Church, the congregation that I had the pleasure of serving in The Bronx, thank you. Special thanks to Eleazar Garza Jr., Nat Perez Jr. and Micah Ransome for your partnership in the Gospel and helping me grow in my imagination of what is possible in Covocational Ministry.

Finally, to the pastors and leaders that I have had the pleasure of serving through I Help Pastors Get Jobs. Thanks for trusting me to be a small part in the redemptive work that God wants to do in and through your ministry. My prayer is this book can encourage, challenge and strengthen God's church to imagine new and fresh possibilities of doing ministry.

To my Lord, Jesus Christ, thank you for calling me to be your disciple, and for shaping me into who You called me to be. May this work be a blessing to those who find it.

Thank you for reading this text and as I mentioned, please e-mail me at eric@ihelppastorsgetjobs.com. I would love to hear your story.

Bibliography

360Learning. "Learning and Development Career Path: Everything You Need to Know." 360Learning. Accessed June 21, 2024. https://360learning.com/guide/learning-and-development-career-path/learning-and-development-career-path/.

Barna Group. "Pastors Are Quitting Ministry." Barna Group. Accessed June 21, 2024. https://www.barna.com/research/pastors-quitting-ministry/.

Nieuwhof, Carey. "Some Thoughts on the Life, Death, and Legacy of Tim Keller." CareyNieuwhof.com. Accessed June 21, 2024. https://careynieuwhof.com/some-thoughts-on-the-life-death-and-legacy-of-tim-keller/.

Rainer, Thom S. "5 Reasons to Be a Co-Vocational Pastor." NewChurches.com. Accessed June 21, 2024. https://www.newchurches.com/resource/5-reasons-to-be-a-co-vocational-pastor/.